C000199226

The HAPPY Labradoodle

Raise a Happy, Well-Mannered Dog and Avoid Dog Behaviour Professionals for Life

- 🐾 Happiness Tips
- 🐾 Techniques for a Well-behaved Labradoodle
- 🐾 Prevent Behaviour Issues
- 🐾 Fulfil Your Puppy's Needs
- 🐾 Be the Ideal Guardian
- 🐾 Avoid Common Mistakes

Asia Moore
Dog Behaviour Expert & Acclaimed Author

Copyright © 2021

Author: Asia Moore
www.K-9SuperHeroesDogWhispering.com
www.KnowsToNose.com
www.MustHavePublishing.com
www.AskBoris.com

Editor & Researcher: Alex Warrington, Ph.D.

Published by:
Worldwide Information Publishing
Middlesex, London
Great Britain
2021

ALL RIGHTS RESERVED. This book contains material protected under International and Federal Copyright Laws and Treaties.

Any unauthorized reprint or use of this material is strictly prohibited. No part of this book may be reproduced or transmitted in any form or by any means, electronic, mechanical or otherwise, including photocopying or recording, or by any information storage and retrieval system without express written permission from the author.

"Dogs are small rays of light caught on the Earth a short time to brighten our days."
— Unknown

Preface

It takes commitment, consistency, tenacity, time, knowledge and firm, vigilant energy to raise a happy and healthy Labradoodle that doesn't suffer from behavioural or stress-related health issues.

This book is atypical from most other breed-specific books, because we believe that it's far better for all parties concerned (human and canine) to **prevent** problems rather than being tormented with the frustrations of living with or learning how to eliminate problems and rehabilitate a Labradoodle that has already developed health or unwanted behavioural issues.

Of course, it's always better to prevent unwanted practices, rather than to hope that you, or someone else, may have what it takes to eliminate them sometime in the future, after your dog has been deemed aggressive or dangerous, your neighbors wish you'd move, your friends no longer visit, your family is at their wits end, and you're having guilty thoughts of re-homing every time you drive past your local SPCA.

 If you want a happy, well-mannered canine companion to be a loyal, well-behaved and valued member of your family, it absolutely DOES matter how you raise your dog and if you

have the right energy for the particular dog you have chosen.

Every breed has uniquely different talents and every dog within a breed may have different talents and needs that are specific to him or her. Even those that were once primarily bred to be working dogs (such as the parents of the Labradoodle) that have now become companion breeds.

As an example, the Border Collie is a very intelligent, high-energy working dog that excels at many different jobs requiring a high-activity level, such as herding. Therefore, if you expect this dog to sleep on the couch all day while you're at work, you will most likely return to ripped up baseboards, chewed up carpets and a once tidy home that looks like it's been invaded by a gang of thieves looking for hidden treasures.

On the other hand, the regal Shih Tzu lap dog, that was originally only permitted to be owned by the wealthy aristocracy, spent their days being pampered, sat on elegant silk pillows, and was used to warm beds and provide comfort. This dog has vastly different daily exercise requirements, and would be a poor choice for someone whose lifestyle called for a canine companion that could protect them from being assaulted by rioters on streets ravaged by marauding gangs.

The highly active and intelligent Labradoodle is a combination of two versatile working breeds that is usually seen as a service canine or a friendly companion for many humans.

 While Wally Conron of Australia initially was credited for naming the Labradoodle in 1989, this mixed breed has been

The Labradoodle crossbreed, whose ancestors include the Labrador Retriever and Poodle breeds, was first officially created to develop a guide dog for the visually impaired who suffered from allergies associated with other breeds.

When combined with their naturally active nature, this friendly fur friend will require plenty of physical and mental stimulation, involving long walks as well as games and trick training so that they do not become bored, overweight and develop unwanted behaviours, such as persistent barking.

Considered to be of above-average intelligence and a quick learner, the happy Labradoodle is generally a friendly, loving and energetic companion. He or she will also most likely be a highly alert watchdog that will get along well with children so long as they are well socialised early in their life.

FACT *A Labradoodle named "Fang" had a recurring TV role on the popular Get Smart sitcom that first aired in 1965.*

In order to raise a happy and healthy Labradoodle fur friend, you need to be totally honest with yourself and absolutely certain that you have the lifestyle and energy needed to properly train, socialise and responsibly care for this friendly and energetic canine companion. Without a confident human to lead them, this active and very smart dog may quickly learn how to rule the roost, which can get you both into a lot of trouble.

In a best-case situation, with a well-bred dog and a guardian who does everything right, you can expect the Labradoodle to be an athletic, energetic, loyal, and loving companion that will be an excellent watchdog.

If this strong-willed, independent-minded dog is bored or under-exercised, and does not respect you as their leader, they may learn to bark at every little noise, or try to escape the yard at every opportunity.

In other words, if this intelligent, robust dog is permitted to rule the roost, they will take on this role with serious conviction and may develop an enthusiastic, barking problem or the reputation for roaming that might cause problems with your neighbours.

While the Labradoodle can vary in temperament from dog to dog, much will depend on their early training and socialisation, as well as the energy of their human guardian.

For instance, some may love everyone they meet, while others may be reserved and wary of strangers. Without proper socialisation and plenty of daily exercise, this dog may become really bored.

When considering sharing your life with this breed, conscientious guardians need to fully understand that this dog needs plenty of physical and mental exercise, and if their humans do not provide this type of opportunities, the guardians in this dog's life can actually be the cause of creating unwanted problems.

This is a highly alert, intelligent, affectionate, energetic, fun-loving, clever and sometimes stubborn dog that will not only enjoy plenty of exercising, without it they may quickly become overweight.

You will want to keep in mind that the Labradoodle comes combining two dogs that both have a long history of being used to hunt and retrieve. This means that he or she may be highly motivated to chase and retrieve.

DID YOU KNOW? *Although the first Labradoodle was a large breed dog and they were originally bred with a Standard Poodle, because the Poodle is bred in three distinctively different sizes, the Labradoodle could also be a Labrador Retriever bred with a Miniature or Toy-sized Poodle.*

While some dogs may greet strangers in a friendly manner, although not usually aggressive, others may be much more wary of people they do not know. While the Labradoodle can be a superior watchdog, you will need to ensure that you do not permit them to get out of control, or take matters into their own paws, and for instance, try to bite the mailman they may think is invading their personal space.

While some Labradoodles have very little natural guarding instinct, others may have a strong guarding instinct. Depending on the particular temperament of the dog you choose, if you are not a strong enough leader and permit him or her to believe that they must protect you, as they become adults, they may display protective aggression toward strangers and other dogs, which could place both of you in a dangerous situation.

This is a strong and agile dog with great stamina that will appreciate an activity-filled lifestyle that involves running, hiking, biking or participating in endless canine sports with their family. He or she may be the perfect companion for an active family with someone who works at home, or is retired, so long as they are firm and consistent with rules and boundaries so that this dog never questions that you are the boss.

 This dog will quickly gain weight if their guardian does not provide him or her with a routine that includes regular vigorous daily exercise.

Every dog breed has unique talents and requirements and when you make the decision to share your life with a particular breed, if you want a well-adjusted, obedient and happy companion, you must provide your dog with what he or she needs to be a valued member of your family.

 Almost all canine problems, both mentally and physically, are a direct result of mismatched energy levels, lack of leadership, knowledge, time or unwillingness on the part of the human guardian to choose the right dog for their particular energy and lifestyle. It takes research, time and commitment to learn what each dog truly needs.

This book offers an uncommon perspective, and humans reading it need to clearly understand that the content of this book is not especially concerned with describing how to eliminate problematic canine behaviours that have already occurred.

Rather, the main focus of this breed-specific book is to explain important details about the breed and then set out what the human guardian needs to commit to providing on a daily basis in order to match the Labradoodle's needs, so that they can raise a happy, healthy and well-behaved dog that never has to experience behavioural issues.

Using the Labradoodle hybrid as a guide or service dog was not common practise until 1989 when Australian breeder Wally Conron first introduced this cross-breed to the Royal Guide Dog Association of Australia. At this time, it was hoped that combining the non-shedding coat of the Poodle with the gentle trainability of the Labrador Retriever, would result in the creation of a guide dog that would be better suited for humans who suffered from allergies to dog fur and dander.

Do not expect this book to be like all the others that set out endless correlations between specific mal-behaviours and various steps or actions the human guardian can take in an attempt to correct them.

In other words, this book is a totally new slant on raising a happy and healthy Labradoodle, because the main focus here is on the <u>prevention</u> of unwanted issues rather than addressing them after they have already surfaced.

"Dogs make humans feel special."
~Asia Moore~

Table of Contents

Chapter 1: Introduction

*"Properly trained, a man
can be dog's best friend."*
— Corey Ford

The purpose of this book is to focus on the essential steps that humans truly need to be aware of when bringing a dog into their life and what they need to commit to providing in order to ensure that this loving companion can live a happy and healthy life. Taking the time to learn these steps will help to ensure a harmonious relationship for everyone.

Even though humans and dogs have been depending on one another for more than 30,000 years, it's still highly important when adding a dog to your family that you first take an honest look at your life. This needs to be a carefully thought-out process, so that you can truly decide whether sharing your life with a dog is feasible. If it is, also equally important will be choosing the right fur comrade that is best suited to your particular energy and lifestyle, because choosing carefully will provide you with the best opportunity for a happy relationship.

Within the pages of this book, you will find tips, facts and information to help you better understand this breed and whether or not YOU have the right energy for raising a happy and well-mannered Labradoodle companion.

In addition, this book describes in detail what the human side of this relationship needs to keep in mind and commit to providing on a daily basis in order to match this bright, energetic and highly trainable companion's needs, so that they can raise a happy, healthy and well-behaved dog that never has to experience behavioural issues.

All the information, suggestions, tips and advice given in this publication is the result of more than 40 years' experience helping many humans positively and effectively interact with the canine world.

If you take all that is written within these pages to heart, and regularly and routinely apply what you've learned, your active and devoted Labradoodle will be a happy family member that will not have to suffer from any behavioural problems. In other words, this book places the **focus on prevention**, rather than attempting to correct troublesome issues after they have already surfaced.

Every Chapter of this book contains valuable information that will provide you with a concrete understanding of the breed and what's involved in raising a happy and well-behaved companion.

For instance, **Chapter 2** – *"Asia's Happiness Tips"* sets out a summary of what she personally believes makes for a happy Labradoodle and encourages you to ask yourself what YOU think would make this dog happy.

Chapter 3 – *"Overview of the Happy Labradoodle"* will outline vital statistics, coat colours and common features, intelligence, temperament and interesting secrets and facts that may not be commonly known.

Further, in order to raise a contented dog, it's important to have some basic knowledge of the interesting history of the Labradoodle breed, so that you are able to better comprehend what this dog's needs might be.

Chapter 4 – *"Healthy Labradoodle = Happy Dog"* is where you will learn about medical care, safety and health issues that may affect this breed, including common diseases and viruses, allergies and canine CPR procedures that could save a life. Needless to say, if your dog is not physically healthy, he or she will not be a happy canine companion for very long, because suffering from health-related issues will undoubtedly create a miserable and ill-mannered dog.

In **Chapter 5** – *"Let Your Dog BE a Happy Dog"*, you will find information about how to let your Labradoodle actually BE a dog, rather than attempting to turn them into a little fur-covered human, which can make for a very confused, unhappy and ill-mannered canine.

Chapter 6 – *"Every Happy Labradoodle Wants Exercise"*, first outlines some of the original history of this dog when they were originally created as working vermin exterminators that have now become companions for humans.

When you are aware of what this breed was originally bred to do, you will have a better understanding of how important it is to commit to the daily exercise routines recommended in this book, without which this energetic fur friend will not be happy or healthy for very long.

Chapter 7 – *"Feeding the Happy Labradoodle"* is where you will find information and ideas about the various food options and feeding suggestions as well as treats to avoid that will assist you in raising a happy and healthy companion.

In **Chapter 8** – *"Care of the Happy Labradoodle",* you will find travel safety tips, licensing, insurance, and important grooming guidance that includes care of nails, ears, teeth and paws, all of which will help you to raise a happy and healthy dog.

Some of this information might seem universal and is quite common sense, however, imagine how you might feel if for instance you had to function for months without washing your hair, trimming your nails or brushing your teeth. Regrettably, that is the normal for many dogs, because their owners have not been aware of the importance of good grooming habits. How happy and well behaved do you think such a poorly cared for dog would be?

Chapter 9 – *"Are YOU the Ideal Labradoodle Guardian?"* is concerned with asking yourself some serious questions, as well as whether your energy, daily activity, time commitment and lifestyle matches what this energetic and affectionate dog needs on a daily basis to be happy and well behaved. It's vital for you to give thoughtful consideration to these questions when considering this (or any) breed, because should you choose the wrong dog to share your life with, it's not just the dog that will suffer the consequences.

Chapter 10 – *"Humans Can Make Mistakes"* outlines that far too often we humans, without even realizing it, can be the cause of creating behavioural problems in our canine companions. Here you will learn some of the common oversights to avoid (and the right thing to do!) when it comes to socialisation, accidental rewards, fear of noises, the safest collars, basic rules and boundaries, adolescent craziness and more.

TIP *Simply being aware of the many accidental blunders we humans can often be guilty of when raising our canine companions, can mean the difference between a Happy Labradoodle with no behavioural issues or a lifetime of frustration and correction.*

Chapter 11 – *"Happy Labradoodle Body Language"*, outlines the foundation of learning canine body language, and will help you be more aware of what's really going on around other dogs. Learning to properly "read" a dog's intentions can prevent an unwanted encounter with another dog or human, and this will help everyone to remain safe and happy.

In Chapter 12 – *"Training Basics for a Happy Labradoodle"*, you will learn helpful training tips and routines that will help to keep your dog truly happy and well behaved for their entire life. It's no surprise that a well-trained dog will be a much happier companion that everyone enjoys being around, and a happy, well-trained dog will be far less likely to develop unwanted behaviour issues somewhere down the road.

Developing a basic training program and learning to teach your dog commands and discipline that establishes a strong bond of trust and respect between human and canine is all part of starting your dog off on the right paw.

Chapter 13 – *"What If You Slip Up?"* is only necessary because we humans tend to get too engrossed, distracted and overwhelmed with day-to-day living, which means we sometimes forget or become too busy to be consistent with providing what our particular dog may need to be happy. If you slip up, this Chapter has outlined a few of the more common behavioural issues and how to promptly get yourself back on track.

Chapter 14 – *"Surprise Bonus Chapter"* is a Question & Answer section containing a few human/canine scenarios with humans asking questions and wise words from the perspective of the dog, who will answer the questions. You will also find a humorous and educational true story about a stubborn dog that refused to set one paw on the newly installed, smooth and shiny tiles in his family home.

Take heed humans, because when you honestly assess your own abilities, compatibility, lifestyle, time commitment and energy level for being the right guardian for the Labradoodle, and are consistent about following the advice and tips outlined in the following pages, you most certainly will be able to raise a healthy and happy dog that will be a joy to share your life with and will never have to suffer from any behavioural issues.

Chapter 2: Asia's Happiness Tips

"Dogs do speak, but only to those who know how to listen."
— Orhan Pamuk

The following few paragraphs are a summary of my own personal ramblings, ideas and beliefs about what I think makes for a happy and contented Labradoodle.

While I hope you may entirely agree, it's absolutely fine if you have other ideas, or if you may have an entirely different take on this subject, because while we may all have our own "personal" ideas about what might make a Labradoodle happy, if your ideas are different from mine, this does not mean that they are any less valid.

While you may gain a little insight from my own personal beliefs, if you're considering sharing your life with this highly intelligent and energetic canine, it's time to take a moment, sit down and consciously think about what would make this particular designer dog truly happy. I encourage you to take the time to carry out this simple exercise and if you have a family, get them involved in this fun exercise, too.

When you sit down with a piece of paper and pen and begin to write down what YOU think would make this dog happy, you may be surprised about what surfaces, and this simple exercise may inspire you and your family to discover new ways to bond with your dog, which will be the basis of a solid and truly happy relationship.

I'll help to get you started with the following question:
"What do you think would make a Labradoodle happy?"

I've shared the last 15 years of my life with a wonderfully loving and well-behaved Shih Tzu and I believe that the very best start you can make, with respect to "happiness" when first bringing home your new puppy is to do all you can to reassure him or her that they are not alone (see below).

Happy New Surroundings

Any puppy will be understandably timid and nervous about the new and unfamiliar faces, smells and surroundings, and will be anxious and missing their mother, other siblings and everything in their environment they had grown used to during their first 8 to 10 weeks of life.

Be careful that you don't overwhelm your new puppy with too much all at once. For instance, close off rooms that you don't need access to and encourage your puppy to come to you as you wander about in a smaller space.

Happy Sleep Patterns

When it's time to go to bed, take your puppy outside for a bathroom break, and then make sure that you have a nice, cozy kennel all ready for your new puppy with a soft lining or blanket, a toy and a treat and place their new kennel inside your bedroom, so that they will be able to hear and see you.

 Unless you want your companion to sleep on your bed when they're fully grown, even when they may have wet or dirty feet, or just rolled in a dead rat, now is the time to exercise a little tough love as the new puppy will most likely not want to be alone in their kennel and will prefer sleeping next to you.

If your bed is large enough to accommodate their kennel, this is the best way to help him or her have a happy sleep time in their new surroundings, because they will be next to you, but still safe inside their own kennel, and as they grow larger, they will be used to their kennel and will not mind that it is sitting on the floor. Congratulations! You've just created a routine that will ensure happy and respectful sleeping patterns for your dog.

Happy Puppy Play

Taking the time for regular play sessions with your new puppy will certainly make them very happy, so make sure you set aside several times during your day when you stop with the human work and chores and engage your puppy in fun games for 5 or 10 minutes several times a day.

 Never let this puppy win when you're playing a tug game, because you want to establish early on (before they are overly strong) that you are the boss and they must always accede to your will.

Happy Puppy Housetraining

One of the very first things your new puppy needs to learn is where the bathroom is, and the more observant and watchful YOU are, the fewer "accidents" will occur, which will make both of you much happier.

I taught my Shih Tzu (Boris) to ring a little bell whenever he needed to go outside, which is a very valuable "trick" to teach. Just hang a loud ringing bell at the end of a ribbon, string or rope from the doorknob of the door (or next to it) where you will always take your dog to go outside for a bathroom break. Every time you take them out, go to the bell, lift their paw and knock it against the bell to make it ring. Say *"Good boy, or girl – go pee?"* Then immediately take them out through this door.

When you learn to pay attention, be observant and understand your dog's body language, you can help teach them proper bathroom habits at a very young age. This is an intelligent dog that wants to please and it should not be difficult to quickly train them that outside is where they need to go to get to their bathroom.

When they wake up in the morning, take them outside immediately. Twenty minutes after they have eaten a meal, take them outside to relieve themselves. After a play session or when they've had a big drink of water, or woken up from a nap, again take them outside. After they've gone pee or number 2, immediately praise and reward them with a treat. Always take them out the same door, and in case they try to take themselves out this door when nobody is paying attention, leave a pee pad at the door.

Yes, to do this correctly, you and your puppy will be spending a lot of time going outside together, but once their bladder grows larger and stronger, the number of hours he or she can "hold" it will increase, and the number of times your dog will have to visit the great outdoor bathroom during each day will become much less.

Take advantage of this bathroom training time, as it can be a perfect way to create a strong bond between you and your dog while also being their first lessons in leash and reward training for doing what you ask and being an obedient follower.

When you go out with them while they're on leash, it's easy to train your dog to "go" on command, and as they mature, you'll be very glad that you took the time to do this, especially if you live in a climate that has cold or wet winters.

Happy Puppy Feeding

We all know that providing your puppy or dog with the best nutrition from the very first day you bring them home will produce a healthier fur friend, which in turn, will lead to a feel-good, energetic and happy companion.

Be aware of the consequences of what you feed your dog and commit to doing the best you can to keep your canine friend healthy and happy. Read labels and feed them only the highest-quality food, so they have the best opportunity for a long life.

While it's important to start your puppy off with the correct food for their growth stages, it's just as important to continue to feed your adult dog the very best diet. Please refer to Chapter 7 (Feeding the Happy Labradoodle), where you will gain an insight into types of food, appropriate treats and more.

<u>Happy Socialising</u>

Socialising a new puppy is one of the most important steps you can take to ensure that your chosen companion lives a happy and stress-free life.

When you don't take the time to properly socialise your puppy, and indeed, keep on socialising throughout their lifetime, you can actually create many behavioural issues, some of which can be so severe that your dog may be in danger of having their life prematurely shortened.

For instance, while the Labradoodle is usually a friendly dog, without socialisation even the friendliest canine can learn to become a dominant and confrontational character that could have a stubborn streak or a willful mind of his or her own. If you pair this up with a mild-mannered human guardian that does not recognize the importance of providing proper socialising and firm rules and boundaries, this dog may soon learn to rule the roost. In this type of situation, rather than the dog learning to be a trustworthy, calm follower, he or she may quickly take on the role of pack leader, which could place both of you into unwanted situations.

Many times, I've been called upon to help a human alleviate aggressive tendencies being displayed by their canine companion. In almost all instances, this type of outcome could have been entirely avoided if a relationship of trust and respect had been established that included teaching firm rules and boundaries early on. You can never discount the importance of proper training and socialising any dog from the get go, and this is even more important with a larger breed.

Every dog needs a human leader to keep them safe and teach them appropriate rules and boundaries, and some dogs such as the Labradoodle, require a firm lead from their human counterparts. Most dogs also require a significant amount of socialising, and more daily exercise and mental stimulation than you might imagine.

 If you socialise well and keep this dog exercised and mentally stimulated every day, there will be much less chance of boredom barking, destructive behaviour or escape attempts.

The Labradoodle will need to be well and continually socialised at a young age, and taught to keep their enthusiasm or boundless energy under control. They will be interested participants that enjoy being involved in all of the family's activities, especially if they involve hiking, running, swimming, learning tricks, a canine sport, or plenty of varied outdoor adventures.

reminder *When not properly socialised, trained and taught to respect the word of their human guardians, this strong and determined companion may soon become a bossy leader if their human's energy is not strong enough for this dog to respectfully follow.*

Without a human to trust, respect and follow, any dog can get into all sorts of unwanted troubles. Keep in mind that without a strong enough leader, any dog may feel forced into being the alpha. When a dog is left to make human decisions, this can often result in the dog being overly protective of their human followers, resulting in him or her acting out in an aggressive manner.

Any sort of aggression is a huge stress on both dog and human and, as we are all aware, stress shortens lives and prevents anyone from experiencing happiness. Help make your dog happy by being a strong and confident leader for him or her, rather than allowing the very heavy burden of making human decisions rest on the shoulders of your best fur friend.

While early socialisation of a puppy is very important, keep in mind that it's just as important to continue socialisation of a grown dog throughout the course of his or her entire lifetime. Please refer to Chapter 10 (Humans Can Make Mistakes) that outlines the many aspects of socialising your Labradoodle.

Happy Training

Almost as important as ongoing proper socialising for helping to keep your dog safe and happy, is proper training, which should never be overlooked. Without training, you may be responsible for creating a dominant, unstable fur friend that ignores their humans, barks, displays aggression, and thinks they are the boss of all they survey.

The very smart Labradoodle is a highly intelligent, intensely eager, and highly versatile dog that will enjoy learning routines, tricks and canine sports.

This alert, eager to please, highly trainable companion has become a popular choice as a family companion, and may enjoy participating in many different canine sports, such as Agility or Dock Diving.

 *Labradoodles are now widely used as assistance, guide and therapy canines worldwide.*

With the right guardian, this intelligent dog could easily become a top performer in the trick training arena and many other popular canine sports. In order to maintain their health, regular daily mental and physical exercise is required that includes learning interesting routines that will prevent their tendency to become overweight, which can lead to health problem issues.

Depending on how curious they may be, how much exercise they normally receive outside of the home, and how strong their prey drive, when not properly trained, this dog may ignore calls to come back when they are on the scent of something interesting.

Begin training this companion as soon as you bring him or her home from the breeder and you will have given yourself the best opportunity to have a happy, eager to comply and safe companion at your side before they are six months old. Of course, you will start out with short training sessions of no more than 5 to 10 minutes at a time, and as they slowly mature, you can increase the length of your sessions.

All training sessions should be a fun and happy time for both you and your dog, with plenty of happy praise and treats, so that he or she will quickly learn to trust and respect you as their leader and be eager for their next session. This loyal, energetic fur friend is loving and friendly with their human family and will be an easy to train dog that should catch on very quickly.

While this smart puppy can begin training at an early age, when you continue their training throughout their life, this companion will usually be an eager participant that is entirely capable of learning many commands, tricks, routines, and hand signals, as well as several canine sports. See more in Chapter 12 (Training Basics for a Happy Labradoodle).

The Labradoodle is a strong and agile dog that will appreciate an activity-filled lifestyle that involves biking, hiking, running or participating in canine sports and outdoor activities with their human family.

 If this dog escapes the home or yard, they may entertain themselves by visiting the neighbors down the street or raiding garbage cans.

Happy Exercising

While the Labradoodle is highly intelligent and versatile, and they enjoy learning new routines, they also need some down time, or some time off from your vigilant supervision.

 Just like us humans, who need time where they don't have to think about work, our dogs also need some free time where they can enjoy romping and playing with the family or exploring and sniffing the local woodland paths, rolling in the grass or lazing in the warm sunshine, and just being a dog.

Depending on their age, the Labradoodle will usually be an energetic dog with a lively and playful temperament that loves to chase and romp, and will be most happy and contented when their day includes much activity. For instance, this dog may be a great hiking companion or a blue-ribbon performer in many different canine sports.

Supervision during play with other dogs is always important with any puppy and in order to prevent possible squabbles or traumatic experiences, you will need to ensure that you are fully in control and capable of intervening to quickly shut down any unwanted situation should your puppy or young dog try to be overly bossy with other dogs or vice versa.

While each dog is different, with respect to how much exercise they might need, how active <u>YOU</u> are will also have a profound effect. Learn much more about the exercises that will keep this dog happy in Chapter 6 (Every Happy Labradoodle Wants Exercise).

<u>Happy Vet Visits</u>

Of course you will want to buy your dog the best food, ensure they receive adequate daily exercise and mental stimulation, properly socialise and carefully train them to be a calm and obedient member of your family, and beyond this you will also want to schedule yearly visits to your chosen veterinarian's office to make sure all is well.

Get your dog used to trips to the vet's office even before they have any real reason to be there. This way they can get used to unfamiliar smells, receive a friendly greeting and perhaps a treat from staff. When you do this, visits will be much less stressful for your dog because he or she will have learned to associate visits to the vet's office as a happy experience.

While it's ideal to get your puppy used to visits to the vet's office early in their life, there is much you can do throughout the life of your adult dog that will help to keep visits for health problems to a minimum. Be sure to read Chapter 8 (Care of the Happy Labradoodle) that outlines many things you can do to help ensure your dog remains as healthy as possible.

Back to the pen and paper exercise.

When you're a caring and observant guardian, and take the time to ponder the many things you can do to raise a happy companion, even more ideas will surface along the way to help you and your chosen fur friend enjoy a long and happy life together. Take my word for it, and *do make the time for this fun exercise* because you will thank me later.

In a Nutshell

The above paragraphs are a short synopsis of what I personally think makes for a Happy Labradoodle, and I'm sure you may have many more ideas to contribute to this list.

The following Chapters of this book contain much more detail concerning what every caring and mindful guardian needs to commit to, on a daily basis, in order to ensure that the human family and their chosen canine companion have the best possible opportunity for enjoying a safe, happy and healthy life together.

Anyone concerned about raising a Happy canine companion that is a joy to share their life with, will want to carefully read through the subsequent Chapters, while always keeping in mind, not just what makes you and your family happy, but also what makes your dog truly happy.

Chapter 3: Overview of the Happy Labradoodle

"If I could be half the person my dog is,
I'd be twice the human I am."
— Charles Yu

It cannot be stressed strong enough how crucial it is that you familiarize yourself with the basics of any breed you may be considering sharing your life with. This will include history, size, energy level, intelligence, temperament, exercise requirements and any special needs. Only once you've made yourself familiar with the basics, can you can truly discern if you are the best individual or family for sharing your life with a particular breed of dog.

In the case of the friendly Labradoodle, this means gaining some basic knowledge of the history of both parent breeds (Labrador Retriever and Poodle) that make up this hybrid companion.

Learning where this dog originally came from will help you choose wisely to ensure that your lifestyle and daily routine can meet this dog's needs.

What About the Labrador Retriever?

The large breed Labrador Retriever (Labrador or Lab) is the most popular dog worldwide, having held the American Kennel Club most popular dog breed record for more than 20 years in a row.

The Lab was originally named the St. John's Water Dog, this dog was originally a working dog that was used to retrieve fishing nets.

This dog became a hunting and waterfowl retrieving purebred gun dog with a long history and was renamed the Labrador Retriever (after the Labrador Sea in Newfoundland, Canada) when they were first imported to England.

Development of the modern Labrador Retriever is attributed to breeding practices of many dedicated Earls, Dukes and Lords who further developed this dog for duck hunting purposes on their estates during 19th century England, with the first Canadian dog believed to have arrived in England during 1820.

Apparently, the Earl of Malmesbury was so impressed with this dog's skill at retrieving anything in the water that once importing several dogs, he then devoted his entire kennel to stabilizing and further developing the Labrador breed.

Approved breed colors are black, yellow or chocolate with a sturdy, muscular body, long, broad tail, long ears, webbed toes and a water-resistant coat for superior swimming and keeping warm in cold water. Interestingly, puppies of all three colors can appear in one litter.

The Labrador retriever coat is short and straight and while they will shed heavily twice a year, they will also shed all year round. This dog tends to have a distinctly "doggy" smell about them.

- A Labrador stands between 21½ and 24½ inches (54 and 62 centimeters) at the shoulder and can weigh between 55 and 80 pounds (24 and 36 kilograms).

- The water-loving Lab is athletic, energetic, playful and most usually friendly to everyone, including all ages of children.

- The enthusiastic Labrador Retriever also has a superior sense of smell, which is why they are often used as detection dogs for hunting down drug smugglers or explosives, among other things.

- This dog is often seen working as a service dog for the blind or hard of hearing or in other areas of service or therapy.

- The American Kennel Club (AKC) recognized the Labrador retriever as a registered breed during 1917, and the Labrador was recognized as an official purebred canine in the United Kingdom in the year1903.

While the Labrador Retriever is an extremely enthusiastic, boisterous, intelligent, easy to train dog with a large personality, that can be high energy, they are also gentle around children and older people.

This is a highly alert and enthusiastic dog that enjoys eating and activity of any sort. This dog can excel in canine sports such as Agility and Obedience, Flyball, Water Retrieving or Dock Diving.

When combined with their naturally active nature, this furry companion will require plenty of physical exercise to prevent them from becoming obese, as well as continued mental stimulation, involving long walks, runs or swimming. In addition, games and other types of training are beneficial so that they do not become bored and develop unwanted behaviours, such as chewing anything they can find.

The Labrador Retriever has a reputation for being always hungry and its strong sense of smell will alert this dog to any potential food source, edible or otherwise. Conscientious guardians will need to carefully oversee the feed bowl and exactly what this dog puts in its mouth to ensure that Labrador does not become overweight.

The Labrador is a friend to all with enough energy and enthusiasm to run and play fetch or swim for hours every day. If this intelligent dog does not receive plenty of daily exercise beyond just a sedate walk around the block, they will soon become overweight and extremely bored. This is a dog that is eager to please and although rambunctious, when training begins early in their life, will be easy to train.

As a result of their boundless energy and their larger size, they are not a particularly good choice for living in an apartment or smaller living space, because they tend to knock things over with their excited clumsiness and strong, whipping tail when in confined spaces.

This is a dog that needs wide-open spaces where they can run, play and fetch. The Lab will love to go running or jogging and hiking with their guardians and if there is a body of water nearby, you will have difficulty keeping them out of it.

What About the Poodle?

You need to know that the friendly, intelligent, fun loving, and active Poodle is one of the smartest dogs in the canine purebred lineup. Originally a working dog, the Poodle was bred and developed in both Germany and Russia for field hunting, which involved retrieving downed waterfowl in the water.

Poodles have been used for a variety of jobs throughout history as hunters and retrievers, circus dogs, and court and companion dogs for the rich and powerful. Despite the Poodle's origins as a hunting and retrieving breed, they became well known for their abilities as performing dogs, and were widely distributed due largely to traveling gypsies who favored the Poodle above all others as a performing circus dog.

The Poodle is not a breed particularly well suited for humans that lead busy lives with long work schedules that keep them away from home. In order for the Poodle to be well-balanced psychologically, they demand a lot of attention and will not be happy spending only a few minutes with their humans each day.

While some breeds of dogs of lower intelligence might be just fine without receiving daily interesting activities to keep them busy and mentally challenged, the Poodle, with their lively and playful temperament, typically wants and needs to occupy much more of their guardian's time and energy by engaging in physical activities that also challenge them mentally.

A Poodle guardian will need to constantly be thinking of ways to challenge their bright and inquisitive canine companion and make their daily life interesting. Otherwise, this intelligent dog may think of ways to entertain themselves that could involve damaging the contents of your home or engaging in barking to vocalize their unhappiness.

The Poodle is a loyal and loving dog that will bond very quickly with any

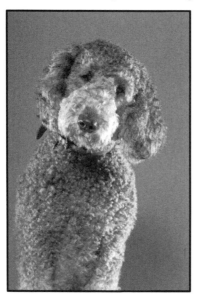

and all family members in a very short period of time. This is a dog that loves being loved, which means that it is very easy for them to be heartbroken when their owners leave them alone.

While the Poodle may be shy around strangers, they rarely act aggressively, and will get along well with other animals in the home, so long as they are slowly and properly introduced to them.

This canine is an enormous people pleaser, who absolutely loves to perform and show off their skills, and they thrive on positive praise and physical affection.

The Poodle is an emotionally sensitivity breed, which means that anyone considering sharing their home with this breed needs to provide them with a peaceful environment. If there is tension in your home, with angry, loud or emotional humans that often get into arguments or fights, this type of home life can literally make them sick to their stomachs, and they may manifest digestive upsets and neurotic behaviours.

When considering sharing your life with the Labradoodle, there are several important points to keep in mind, including:

- they are highly intelligent, requiring plenty of mental and physical daily exercise

- frequent brushing or combing is required to keep their soft silky coat free of mats as well as regular trips to the groomers approximately every six weeks if you want to keep this dog's coat a manageable length

- you need to begin a regular brushing process early so that they calmly accept it as part of their life, especially if you plan on letting them keep a longer coat, because otherwise, you will have to battle to keep your dog looking his or her best.

- they may be a clever escape artist

- they may have an insatiable appetite

- they may gain weight quickly, so do not over feed

History of the Labradoodle

While historians believe that the Labradoodle is a relatively new creation (as compared to purebreds with hundreds of years under their belt), it is thought that once this hybrid became popular during the 1980's in Australia, this was the beginning of the Poodle hybrid craze that is still going strong.

For instance, from the Chihuahua to the Saint Bernard, today there are few purebreds that haven't also been purposefully mixed with the Poodle.

DID YOU KNOW? *It is believed that the name "Labradoodle" was first coined in 1955 by Donald Campbell.*

While the original intention of crossing the Labrador with the Poodle was to create a guide dog that did not provoke an allergic reaction in sensitive humans, the eventual success of this breeding program (started by Wally Conron in Australia) had its share of problems.

Firstly, at the outset of this breeding program, nobody wanted a dog that wasn't purebred, which meant that Conron could not find suitable homes where these hybrid puppies would be socialised.

Next, Conron ran into difficulties when he needed male Poodles with an even temperament to breed with his Labradors. Many breeders were against such a "mixed" program, and the Kennel Club was threatening to remove anyone from their registry if they provided their male dogs for breeding.

Conron was lucky to find some breeders who offered their males so long as it was carried out in secret, and this was how he was able to successfully create Labradoodles that were the perfect guide dog for those with allergies.

Sadly, once the public demand for these dogs became so great that the breeding program could not keep up, unscrupulous, puppy mill breeding farms took over with no care selecting intelligent and easily trained parents that would have been great guide dogs. Rather, any two dogs were bred together without a care to health or temperament, or any testing for hypoallergenic qualities.

DID YOU KNOW? *While the Labradoodle cross breed has been around for a long time, the American Kennel Club and other major kennel clubs do not recognize them as an official breed because they are a mix of two separate breeds.*

Once Conron became tired of being sued and threatened by those pure bred breeders who were adamantly against mixing breeds, he gave up the fight to continue to produce litters that had all the right qualities. Other reputable breeders took up where he left off and today still continue to develop this breed.

FACT *There is an "Australian Labradoodle", that generally differs from the Labradoodle we have come to know, because they may be mixed with other breeds that include both the American and English Cocker Spaniel, curly-coated retrievers, Wheaten Terriers, and two Irish water Spaniels.*

 Many well-known celebrities have shared their lives with the Labradoodle, such as Tiger Woods, Neil Young, Henry Winkler, Joe Biden, and Barbara Eden.

OK, now that you have a basic understanding of the history of this loving, energetic and versatile canine, following is the main overview of the breed, which will be the foundation of wisely choosing and raising a happy and well-behaved dog.

Labradoodle Vital Statistics

While every dog is unique, there are usually standards that are common to each purebred canine, such as height, weight and various coat types, colours and features. You can also get a pretty good idea of what the puppies will look like when full grown, when you see their parents.

Height and Weight

While the original Labradoodle was a Labrador Retriever bred to a Standard Poodle, just like the Poodle, who is recognized for three different sizes (Standard, Miniature and Toy) the Labradoodle has also been bred in smaller sizes. There are now three distinctly different sizes of Labradoodles, including Standard, Medium or Miniature. Sizes can vary between 14 and 22 inches (35 and 56 cm). Average lifespan may range more or less between 12 and 15 years.

Coat Colors and Common Features

While the coat color, size and temperament of the Labradoodle will largely depend upon the appearance and size of both breeding parents, this hybrid canine will tend toward having a non-shedding, softer, fluffier coat that will be more easily tolerated by human allergy sufferers. Note that a coat that is left to grow long will usually grow to be between 4 and 8 inches in length.

When first born, a first-generation Labradoodle puppy will often look very much like a Poodle. Experienced breeders will tell you that shortly after birth, the puppies who will grow up to have long, shaggy coats will start to show crimping or "ripples" in their coats. Those puppies that display the most ripples in their coats will be fluffier with shaggy faces by the time they are just eight weeks old.

When considering this breed, you will want to choose a professional breeder with a good reputation, because popular hybrid dogs often fall prey to the exploitation of inhumane puppy mill breeding, and some more disreputable breeders may be breeding too small, which can cause many health issues and shorten this dog's life.

This athletic, sturdy dog has a deep chest, strong legs, an almost square, compact body, a large square nose and long pendant ears that will be heavily covered in hair.

The eyes are expressive, large, slightly round-shaped and color will usually be hazel to dark brown, depending on the coat color.

The natural tail will be of medium length and carried in a high, sabre shape. Coat colours may include any solid color from black to white with or without small white markings, as well as Parti, Brindle, Sable or Phantom patterns.

 ***The popular Labradoodle has made its way into the Oxford English Dictionary.***

How Smart is the Labradoodle?

Every dog is surprisingly different even within the same breed, and despite what some "experts" might have to say about it, there are *"people smarts"* and *"dog smarts"* and these two ways of rating intelligence are often widely divergent or in conflict with one another.

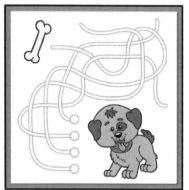 If you really want to rate your dog's intelligence, based on what we humans think is *"smart",* there is a book *("The Intelligence of Dogs")* written in 1994 by Stanley Coren, which has become the standard for rating the intelligence of different canine breeds.

While I can agree, in part, with some of the information contained in this book, I can also disagree. I have much personal experience with many breeds, and while I concur with the rating given for the Labradoodle, I have found that even some dogs that are rated very low on the intelligence scale are also very smart in their own way.

Therefore, I caution you not to pre-handicap your dog's level of intelligence just because of something you may have read in a well-respected book, because each dog has their own unique set of talents and much of how they develop mentally is up to their guardian.

Coren judges canine intelligence of particular purebred canines based on three categories, as follows:

"**Instinctive Intelligence** – *a dog's ability to carry out tasks it was bred to perform, such as guarding, herding, hunting, pointing, retrieving or supplying companionship.*"

"**Adaptive Intelligence** – *how well a dog is able to solve problems on its own.*"

"**Working/Obedience Intelligence** – *how quickly a dog is able to learn from humans.*"

The Labradoodle is a very smart dog that will usually be eager to learn and easy to train so long as you demonstrate to him or her that you have strong enough energy to lead them. Coren places both parents of this smart hybrid dog in the top ten out of 138 listed breeds in the *"Brightest Dogs"* category.

Please keep in mind that there are always exceptions to every study and a particular breed's degree of intelligence is often related to their early upbringing and how they are trained.

I have had personal experience with this breed, and can tell you that they are indeed eager to please and quick to learn. When you are firm with them and use fair and positive training methods that involve treat rewards, this will be an intelligent, versatile and willing to learn dog that will be highly trainable.

When training a puppy, be patient, consistent and no more than 5 to 10 minutes each time. It's important to learn when enough is enough so your puppy doesn't become overwhelmed and simply zone out.

DID YOU KNOW? *A stuffed toy Labradoodle, manufactured by Lord & Taylor, has been used by the American Cancer Society to raise charitable funds.*

If this exuberant dog is misbehaving, it's most likely because they are bored and frustrated, and they need much more exercise. This smart dog needs something to do that stretches their mind and body, and if you don't provide them with consistent, daily, sufficient mental and physical exercise, he or she may become stressed, overweight and unhappy.

Make sure that your training involves fair, firm guidance and discipline and plenty of socialising from a young age, so that he or she will listen to your commands, abide by the rules and boundaries you've taught, and trust and respect you as their leader.

FACT *Any humans that don't have the confidence and sufficient knowledge to properly socialise, train, establish and then consistently enforce rules, may soon find themselves in trouble if they let this super smart dog take the lead.*

Labradoodles are agile and energetic athletes with great stamina that can excel in any sort of advanced training or obedience competition, where retrieving and jumping skills are required, or in Agility (obstacle course) or Flyball competitions, where speed and concentration is required.

Temperament of the Labradoodle

The versatile Labradoodle is an alert, intelligent, affectionate, energetic, fun-loving, clever and sometimes strong-willed dog that will not only enjoy plenty of exercising, this will be essential to their health.

While this breed will likely become very attached, protective and devoted to its family members, they will not usually be aggressive toward strangers or other dogs unless they have not been properly socialised at a young age.

These dogs bond strongly to humans of all ages, and when properly socialised can be social and friendly to everyone they meet along their exciting road of life.

The Labradoodle is a sturdy, yet usually gentle dog with superior hearing that is great for children of all ages. They will be alert and faithful companions always eager for the next adventure.

This is a dog that will really excel when given thinking tasks to accomplish. If their daily routine does not include a sufficient amount of mental and physical exercise, they can become bored, and may create their own entertainment, which can include destroying your property or chronic barking at every little noise.

Taking into consideration both parents of this hybrid dog, as you would expect, the smart and capable Labradoodle will be an active dog that is an impressive jumper, runner and swimmer who will excel at any activity you have the time to engage in.

The Labradoodle will be a good choice for active families with young children, or older adults who have the energy, time and mobility required to give them the daily exercise they need.

This is a dog that can be quite *boisterous (especially when young)* who really needs a structured living situation and a regular exercise routine in order to prevent anxiety and other behavioural problems that may stem from being under-exercised.

This dog loves to play, so a living space that includes a back yard where they can burn off energy chasing a ball or running an Agility course would be ideal.

Unfortunately, sometimes people choose the Labradoodle as a companion based on all the wrong reasons, including:

- 🐾 those pleading puppy eyes
- 🐾 their non or low shedding coat
- 🐾 feeling sorry for a dog surrendered to a rescue or the SPCA
- 🐾 fond childhood memories of a neighbour's dog
- 🐾 their sturdy build and affectionate nature
- 🐾 their best friend has the same breed
- 🐾 their playful and loyal temperament

- their star status from being featured in movies or on TV

To choose any dog as your companion based on looks or other superficial criteria could end up being a BIG mistake that you could regret. In order to choose wisely for yourself or your family, it's a much better idea to consider the intelligence and energetic nature of this breed and their strong desire for plenty of attention and daily mental and physical exercise.

When this dog is chosen for the wrong reasons, once the puppy cute factor has worn off, the unpredictable age of adolescence kicks in, and the family becomes distracted with other areas of their life, the result could inevitably be an unhappy, frustrated and under-exercised dog that suffers from boredom and may soon become destructive, noisy and/or unhealthily overweight.

Any dog that is not routinely challenged by moderate to high daily activity and mental stimulation, especially an intelligent and active one that comes from a working background, may develop problematic behaviours.

Unwanted behaviours with a bored Labradoodle can be many, and as an example may include:

- destructive chewing
- raiding the garbage
- chewing holes in walls
- excessive barking
- chasing the neighbour's cat
- destructive hole digging in your back yard
- escaping the house or yard entirely

TIP ***If you think your dog will be safe left all alone in your fenced back yard, and still be there when you return home, you may need to think again. The Labradoodle is a highly clever, athletic***

companion capable of solving problems, and if bored and given enough time, he or she may figure out how to escape confinement in search of something interesting to occupy them.

The Labradoodle lives for play and adventure and if left alone for long hours they will be very unhappy, which could encourage them to become a talented escape artist. This agile and highly intelligent dog may soon figure out how to open latches or escape from confinement by using their strong legs to jump fences, climb fences, dig under fences or find cracks they can squeeze through if they want to get out.

When this dog is bored and lonely, they usually <u>WILL</u> want to get out because they always want to be with their human family or engaged in some sort of interesting task that puts their intelligence to good use.

When you have a compatible, active lifestyle and are able to keep this smart and sensitive dog at your side throughout the majority of your days, and have the knowledge to teach with a firm, yet kind and consistent approach, he or she will be a highly trainable companion you will be proud to call your best friend.

Every dog needs the discipline of being regularly walked on leash outside of the home each day, as well as the opportunity for off-leash time to run and play fetch or enjoy socialising with other dogs under your close supervision.

When treated fairly and trained with firm, positive reinforcement, this loving and affectionate companion will have a zest for learning new things very quickly and will love the attention any sort of training program provides.

BOTTOM LINE: this boisterous companion will be a happy and contented member of your family so long as you engage them in moderate daily walks, high energy running free time, a vigorous canine sport, or perhaps spend time teaching him or her various tricks and routines.

The athletic and very smart Labradoodle is highly capable of excelling at many different canine sports, and it will be up to their guardian to figure out where their particular talent lies. For instance, flying around an Agility course, being an unbeatable competitor at Dock Diving, jumping high to catch that Frisbee, or even learning how to surf might be this dog's special talent.

Whatever you teach this hybrid, at a minimum, make sure that you always get them outside for several daily, 30-60 minute walks and allow them some off-leash time to freely run, swim, fetch and sniff and learn proper socialising skills with other dogs.

The highest priority for an energetic Labradoodle with a busy mind is always that they are kept engaged with play, vigorous daily exercise, challenging canine sports, and being included in family outings and activities because this also helps to socialise and prevent them from becoming bored.

When they are puppies, it's important to engage this dog in thinking and working activities because they need this mental stimulation as part of their on-going healthy development.

As you can well imagine, how active you are will have a sizeable impact on the health of your Labradoodle. Remember that without sufficient daily activity this dog may soon become lethargic, overweight and unhealthy.

All puppies are energetic, curious bundles of fun, including this puppy, and if you take the time to be active with them at a young age, and engage them in training and activities that stretch their minds and exercise their bodies, chances are that they will continue to be active well into their senior years.

On the other hand, if you are more of a couch potato human, or spend the majority of your days stuck behind a computer screen, the chances are high that this dog will become lazy, overweight, bored and very frustrated, which can lead to unwanted behaviours and exacerbated health problems.

While this brilliant companion can be just as happy living in a rural setting, or enjoying the city lifestyle, keep in mind that he or she may still like to chase birds or small critters, and if you do not find safe ways to regularly address any natural hunting desires, they may display their feelings of frustration through destructive chewing, digging or excessive barking.

Labradoodle Special Needs

This smart dog is affectionate, loving and often protective (in a non-threatening way) with their family. He or she may also be quite sensitive and they will thrive when receiving plenty of close human contact and playful loving interaction with their humans throughout the day.

The Labradoodle is a very intelligent, easy to train dog, which means that for them to be balanced and fulfilled, they will need plenty of mental stimulation in the form of trick training, advanced obedience, canine sports or puzzles where they get to use their brain to figure out problems.

Unlike some other breeds that may appear to be stubborn or seem to have a shorter attention span, this attentive dog is eager to learn and will easily take direction from their human to teach them what is acceptable behaviour and what is not.

This dog will need to have their coat regularly clipped approximately every six weeks, and will require brushing in between to keep their coat free of painful mats.

DID YOU KNOW? *The Labradoodle lives to love their humans and spend plenty of time enjoying bouncy, playful adventures.*

In order to keep the energetic and active Labradoodle happy, they really need *to be engaged in* a wide variety of interesting tasks to keep them busy. Consider teaching this dog many tricks, routines and canine sports that will challenge their doggy smarts and help drain out that boisterous energy.

Never forget about early and on-going socialisation and training so that they don't take over or become possessive of their humans and/or testy with other dogs and animals.

Consider training this spirited, happy dog to jog with you on a "Springer Bicycle Jogger" (**pictured**) that attaches to your bicycle, so they can receive a good amount of vigorous disciplined exercise in a short period of time, while still remaining safely under your control.

Keep in mind that making sure this friendly, energetic athlete is happy and contented may involve much more time and attention than a first-time dog guardian or otherwise busy family is able to provide.

While conscientious breeders are concerned about breeding for intelligent, mild-tempered, well-balanced family companions, as this dog is a combination of two breeds with hunting and retrieving DNA in their background, this canine may still retain more or less of their original chasing and retrieving urges.

Depending on how strong this dog's hunting and chasing instinct may be, how independent-minded they may be, and how well they have been trained, they may decide to chase a bird or wander after an interesting scent when out walking a trail or hiking in unfamiliar areas. However, this dog will be strongly attached to their humans and will usually not roam too far away without returning to check in with their humans.

<u>Happy Labradoodle Secrets</u>

The Labradoodle breed name is a combination of both parent breed names, with the extra "d" added to make it easier to pronounce.

Being a combination of two water-loving breeds, this hybrid will almost certainly love to swim, or retrieve floats from the water, too.

Even mixed breed dogs, like the Labradoodle, can be registered with the American Kennel Club Partner Program, so that they can participate in sports and obedience programs alongside their purebred cousins..

This is a highly intelligent, versatile and attentive dog that literally can do whatever you might have your heart set on doing.

For instance, whether you want your dog to bring home blue ribbons in the Agility ring, jump the farthest in a Dock Diving competition, or learn to hang 16 on a surfboard, this dog is eager to learn and highly capable of mastering any of these, plus many more.

Both an active adventurer and an affectionate companion, the Labradoodle has become a popular breed around the world.

This is a bright and active dog with tireless stamina and if you have the time, patience and determination, there is literally no end to what you could teach the amazing Labradoodle.

FACT *As a result of both of this dog's parents originally being bred to retrieve, offspring may retain a strong attraction to water and fast-moving small creatures or objects, such as balls and Frisbees, which could make this dog a serious competitor in the canine sports of Flyball, Disc Dog or Dock Diving.*

With an energetic guardian, the Labradoodle can be an affectionate, fun-loving, playful, and loyal family companion that could be the perfect dog for an active family.

In a Nutshell

Familiarizing yourself with the hybrid Labradoodle, their parentage, early history and special needs, plus understanding their need for mental stimulation, moderate to high energy levels, eagerness to learn and vigorous exercise requirements will help you to decide if this friendly dog is the right companion for you and your family.

When you take the time to understand your chosen breed's needs, this will not only save you and your dog from much future grief, it will be an important pre-requisite for raising a content, well-behaved, and happy canine that you are proud to call your best friend and companion.

Chapter 4: Healthy Labradoodle = Happy Dog

"Dogs are not our whole life,
but they make our lives whole."
— Roger Caras

If your Labradoodle is not physically healthy, he or she will not be a happy canine companion for very long, because suffering from health-related issues can easily create a miserable and ill-mannered dog.

There are many simple steps you can take to prevent problems from occurring so that you can feel confident that you are doing all that you can to keep on top of your dog's best health, including:

- Choose a veterinarian that can provide yearly check-ups

- Spay or neuter in a timely fashion

- Research a healthy diet for him or her

- Keep on top of regular grooming

- Be aware of issues common to the breed that could adversely affect your dog's health.

As well, take the time to learn a little canine CPR, because doing so may save the life of your dog, or even someone else's.

Below you will find more information that may help you raise a happy and healthy dog.

Choose Your Veterinarian Wisely

Some canine health clinics specialize in caring for smaller pets, while some specialize in larger animal care, and others have a wide-ranging area of expertise and will care for all animals, including livestock and reptiles.

Choosing an appropriate veterinary clinic for your dog will be very similar to choosing the appropriate doctor or health care clinic for your own personal health. You want to feel confident that your fur friend will receive the quality care they deserve, so take some time to find a suitable vet. A good place to begin your search will be by asking other dog owners where they take their furry friends and whether they are happy with the service they receive.

 Take your dog into your chosen clinic several times before they actually need to be there for any treatment, so that they are not fearful of the strange smells and unfamiliar surroundings.

Consider Timely Neutering or Spaying

While opinions may vary regarding the best time to neuter or spay a young dog, many do agree that earlier spaying or neutering, between the ages of 4 and 6 months, can be a more preferable choice than waiting longer.

Non-neutered or spayed males and females are more likely to display aggression related to sexual behaviour, than are dogs that have been neutered or spayed.

As well, fighting, particularly between male dogs, is less common after neutering. Also, the intensity of other types of aggression, such as irritable aggression in females will usually be totally eliminated after spaying, so make that appointment at the vet's office and get it done.

Effects on General Temperament: often we humans become needlessly worried that a neutered or spayed dog will lose their vigour, when in reality, you will be a caring and conscientious guardian when you take action to help diminish or eliminate many undesirable qualities that can be the result of hormonal impact. Be a conscientious guardian, and do your part to help stop accidental litters of puppies.

Effects on Escape and Roaming: a spayed or neutered dog is less likely to be motivated to escape and wander, and male dogs that have been castrated tend to patrol smaller sized outdoor areas and are much less likely to participate in territorial rivalry with other male dogs they may perceive as challengers.

Possible Weight Gain: while metabolic changes that occur after spaying or neutering may cause some puppies to gain weight, often the real culprit for any weight gain is the human guardian feeling guilty for subjecting their puppy to this medical procedure, and in an attempt to make themselves feel better, they feed more treats or meals to their companion.

Also remember that after spaying or neutering, your puppy must not be as active as they previously were for about 10 days, in order to let the stitches properly heal. A temporary reduction in activity level can result in an increase in weight that will usually not be a problem after your dog resumes their normal activity level.

If spaying or neutering your puppy seems to have resulted in weight gain, simply adjust your dog's food and treat intake as needed, and once stitches are healed, make sure that they are receiving adequate daily exercise to maintain a healthy weight.

Educate Yourself About Vaccinations

Currently it has become common practice to vaccinate adult dogs every three years. If your veterinarian is suggesting a yearly vaccination for your dog, ask them why, because more than every three years may be considered by many professionals to be *"over vaccinating"*.

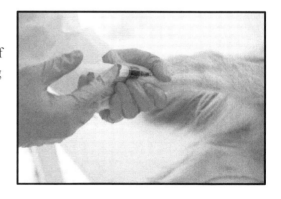

Take an active role in your dog's health, ask questions and with respect to booster vaccinations, before running the risk of over vaccinating, suggest that your vet give your dog a blood test because this is a simple way to determine whether or not he or she actually needs a booster.

It's important for puppies to be vaccinated in order to provide them with protection against four common and serious diseases referred to as **"DAPP"**, which stands for Distemper, Adenovirus, Parainfluenza and Parvo Virus.

Approximately one week after your puppy has completed all three sets of primary DAPP vaccinations, they should be fully protected from those specific diseases.

Be Aware of the Health Conditions That May Affect Your Dog

A healthy, happy Labradoodle may live to be 12 to 15 years (on average), and with a daily routine that provides sufficient mental and physical exercise, regular check-ups and an appropriately nutritious diet they may not suffer from any of the below noted health concerns.

When considering a hybrid for your favorite fur friend, while mixed breeds are often healthier than their parents, it is still advisable to familiarize yourself with all health concerns possibly associated with each of the breed parents.

The following pages will outline problems associated both with the Labrador retriever and the Standard Poodle, so that you have a clear understanding of problems that *"may"* affect your dog.

Health Concerns for both Labrador Retriever & Poodle

Hip & Elbow Dysplasia (pictured for hip): is a degenerative disease in which the hip or elbow joint becomes weakened due to abnormal growth. Depending upon the severity of the disease, treatment will involve medication or

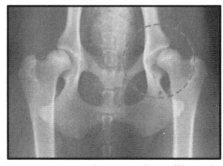

surgery. Screening of the parents cannot guarantee that puppies will not be born with this problem.

This is a musculoskeletal issue commonly seen in many breeds. Dysplasia occurs when the head of the bone slips out of its rightful place in the socket. When the bone is out of joint, it can cause the dog to limp or it might cause total limb lameness. Over time, the wear and tear on the joints can lead to painful inflammation, which may necessitate a surgical repair. In more mild cases, other treatment options include pain medications and anti-inflammatories.

Luxating Patella: This slipping kneecap condition is a common defect seen in many breeds, including the Labrador and Poodle, and can often be caused by accidentally falling or jumping from a height. Often you will see a dog with this problem appear to be skipping down the road as they occasionally lift one leg when the kneecap slips out of the patellar groove and the leg locks up. Surgery is the treatment option for this condition, although many dogs live a relatively normal life with this defect.

Obesity: the Labrador and Poodle are very food motivated, which means that without adequate exercise and too much food intake, they may easily become obese, which can lead to joint problems and heart disease.

Hypothyroidism: is a condition resulting from an inadequate production of thyroid hormone and is treated with medication. Symptoms can include weight gain or obesity, constant hunger, reduced energy and a coarser feel to the dog's coat texture. Blood samples will be taken in order to test for a malfunctioning thyroid.

Progressive Retinal Atrophy (PRA): Some dogs can suffer from several eye problems, including PRA that causes degeneration of the retina, which is the part of the eye that senses visual information and sends it to the brain.

Degeneration of this vital part of the eye eventually will lead to blindness. This disease usually appears between 3 and 5 years of age. A simple DNA test is available to determine without waiting for symptoms to appear.

Cataracts (see picture): like many dogs, the Labrador and the Poodle can suffer from cataracts that cause the lens of the eye to become opaque or cloudy, leading to blindness.

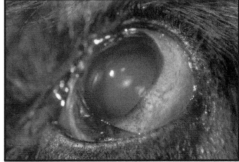

While this disease usually occurs in old age, it can also appear in a younger dog and treatment involves surgical removal.

Unfortunately, cataracts cannot be prevented, especially if it is a condition your puppy inherited genetically. If the cataract is caught while still in the early stages, however, your vet may be able to take steps to slow the progression and may even save your dog's vision. In some cases, a dog's vision can be restored by surgically removing the cataract, however, there is a fairly long recovery period for this kind of surgery.

Ear Infections: as a result of their long hanging ears, these dogs are commonly prone to chronic ear infection or inflammation. Therefore, guardians need to make sure that the ears are kept clean, dry and free of excessive hair growth.

Bloat (Emergency Gastrointestinal Syndrome): is a life-threatening, common occurrence that can affect any size of deep-chested canine. This condition can happen quickly, especially if you feed your dog right after vigorous exercise, or if they are a very fast eater and gulp in large quantities of air with their food. The stomach then distends with gas and fluid which can cause the stomach to twist 180-degrees or more.

von Willebrand Disease (vWD): is a blood disorder similar to hemophilia in humans, where blood does not clot properly, which means that if the dog becomes injured (or during surgery), they are more likely to suffer from excessive bleeding episodes. There is a simple DNA test available to rule out this disease at any time, rather than waiting for symptoms to appear.

Labrador Retriever Health Concerns

Glaucoma (pictured): this eye disease, which is usually caused by an increase of fluid pressure in the eye, can cause permanent damage to the dog's vision in the affected eye or eyes, which, if left untreated, can lead to blindness. The required treatment can be medical (anti-glaucoma eye drops) or surgical (shunt  placement or laser surgery) and the best approach to be followed varies between individual dogs.

Retinal Dysplasia: this eye disease appears as streaks or dots in the retina of the dog's eye, which can lead to blindness.

Corneal Dystrophy: this disease is a change in the eye usually attributed to aging, causing fluid leakage that appears as a bluish color in the inner layer of the cornea.

Lens Luxation: is a dislocation of the lens in the dog's eye, which primarily is seen in dogs between the ages of 4 and 9 years. This luxation occurs when the fibers holding the lens in place break causing the positioning of the lens to shift forward or backward. The result can cause glaucoma and if the condition can be corrected surgically before severe glaucoma occurs, it is possible to save the dog's vision. Dogs suffering from this problem should not be bred.

Hereditary Myopathy: this is a disease of the muscles that causes weakness in the muscle tissues when the fibers of the muscles cease to function. This condition is usually considered to eventually be lethal with the cause often being cited as stress or over exertion of the muscles. Symptoms can include a shortened gait often referred to as *"bunny hopping"*.

Exercise Induced Collapse: exercise Induced Collapse (EIC) usually appears following short periods of strenuous exercise and can display as disorientation, weakness, collapse and hyperthermia.

Dogs affected with this syndrome often are able to tolerate mild or moderate exercise. However, a short period (5 to 20 minutes) of excitement or strenuous activity, which often occurs during hunting tests or field trials, can cause weakness leading to collapse. Dogs with this syndrome can live normal lives so long as they do not continue with intense training routines.

Poodle Health Concerns

Sebaceous Adenitis: is a rare type of inflammatory skin disease, the cause of which is currently unknown, that can cause raw and blistered skin. Signs of this disease may include small clumps of matted hair, a dull and brittle coat, intense itching and scratching, and white scales on the dog's skin. Treatment will depend on the severity of the disease and may include medication, light brushing to remove flaking skin, and medicated shampoos, oils and skin rubs to moisturize and help remove scales.

Epilepsy: Seizures can occur in all three sizes of Poodle and the most common cause is idiopathic epilepsy, which is an inherited form of epilepsy. However, many factors can cause seizures and it is very important to have a dog diagnosed if seizures begin.

Addison's Disease: is a chronic, slowly developing disease that involves a disorder of the adrenal glands, which then results in either insufficient or excessive production of key hormones. It is seen most often in young to middle-aged dogs and typically in more female dogs. In critical situations it can be life threatening.

There are many symptoms including lack of appetite, vomiting, weight loss, tiredness, diarrhea, dehydration, hair loss, increased thirst, lowered temperature, painful abdomen, blood in faces, and collapse. The disease can be controlled with medication that they will require for the rest of their life.

Atrial Septal Defect (ASD): this relatively rare genetic heart problem is a hole between the upper heart chambers. Symptoms may include difficulty breathing, coughing, intolerance to exercise, fainting and death from heart failure. If detected, surgery can repair the hole.

Legg-Calve-Perthes Disease: is a serious, but less common disease of the hip joint causing degeneration of the head of the femur, which leads to severe pain and subsequent lameness.

Many noted health conditions can be prevented when conscientious breeders carefully screen breeding stock so that hereditary or genetic health conditions will not be passed on to the puppies.

When you take good care of your happy Labradoodle's health, and they come from a trusted breeder, he or she may never have to suffer from any of the above-noted list of health problems.

FACT *If your dog is an avid participant in the ball retrieving game, DO NOT use tennis balls because they are made with fiberglass that will wear down your dog's teeth. Instead, choose only balls that are certified safe for dogs.*

Educate Yourself About Common Canine Diseases and Viruses

Even though your dog may never suffer from a common disease or virus, in order to ensure the health and safety of your happy Labradoodle, it's a good idea to be aware of diseases and viruses that could adversely affect your dog's health.

If you recognize symptoms of the following common diseases and suspect that your dog has been infected, you will want to contact your vet immediately.

Distemper (sometimes called *"hard pad disease"*): is a contagious, and deadly viral illness spread through the air or by direct or indirect contact with a dog (or other animal) that is already infected (such as ferrets, foxes, raccoons, skunks and wolves). This illness can also cause thickening of the pads of the feet or the nose.

Early symptoms include fever, loss of appetite and mild eye inflammation that may only last a day or two, and then becoming more serious and noticeable as the disease progresses. There is no known cure.

Adenovirus: causes infectious canine hepatitis, which can range in severity from very mild to very serious. Symptoms can vary and may include increased thirst and urination, tiredness, coughing, loss of appetite, vomiting and seizures. Management of symptoms will be the treatment focus, and the condition can sometimes result in death.

Canine Parainfluenza Virus (CPIV): is also known as *"canine influenza virus"*, *"greyhound disease"* or *"race flu"*, and is easily spread through the air or by coming into contact with respiratory secretions. While usually a self-limiting virus that will run its course within a couple of weeks, in more severe cases and without antibiotic treatment, this virus can be fatal.

Symptoms can include difficulty breathing, wheezing, a dry, hacking cough, runny nose and eyes, sneezing, tiredness, fever, loss of appetite, depression and possible pneumonia. In cases where only a cough exists, tests will be required to determine whether the cause of the cough is the parainfluenza virus or the less serious *"kennel cough"*.

Canine Parvovirus (CPV): is a viral illness that is highly contagious, affecting puppies and dogs, coyotes, foxes, and wolves. Symptoms include lack of appetite, vomiting, weight loss, and bloody diarrhoea. Dogs suffering from severe parvovirus infections can die within 48 to 72 hours if they do not receive prompt and proper treatment.

Proper treatment will involve addressing dehydration and correcting electrolyte imbalances by administering intravenous fluids. Various drugs will be given to control diarrhoea and vomiting, as well as anti-inflammatory and antibiotic drugs to control or prevent septicaemia.

Other Diseases and Viruses to Be Aware Of

What is Zoonotic? Zoonotic means a contagious disease that can be spread between both humans and animals.

Rabies: is a zoonotic, viral disease transmitted through a bite, or by otherwise coming into contact with the saliva of, an infected animal. The virus travels to the brain along the nerves and once symptoms develop (usually noted by a change in temperament), after a lengthy period of suffering, death is almost certainly inevitable. There is no treatment.

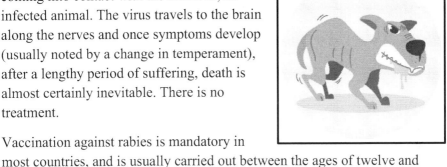

Vaccination against rabies is mandatory in most countries, and is usually carried out between the ages of twelve and sixteen weeks. If you plan to travel out of State or across country borders, you will want to make sure that your dog has an up-to-date Rabies Vaccination Certificate indicating they have been inoculated against rabies.

Leishmaniasis: is a contagious zoonotic infection caused by a parasite and transmitted through a bite from a sand fly. While treatment protocol involves the administration of a special drug (sodium stibogluconate), there is no definitive answer for effectively combating Leishmaniasis (especially since one vaccine will not prevent the known multiple species). Prognosis is often fatal.

Symptoms may include diarrhoea, loss of appetite, vomiting, severe weight loss, being tired and intolerant to exercise, nosebleed, tarry feces, fever, painful joints, excessive thirst and urination, muscle inflammation. and death from kidney failure.

Lyme Disease: is one of the most common zoonotic tick-borne diseases in the world and it is transmitted by Borrelia bacteria found in the deer or sheep tick. The symptoms are many and include recurrent lameness from joint inflammation, loss of appetite, depression, stiff walk with arched back, sensitivity to touch, swollen lymph nodes, fever, and kidney damage, as well as rare heart or nervous system complications.

Control of symptoms and completely eliminating the organism requires a lengthy course of antibiotic treatment.

Rocky Mountain Spotted Fever (RMSF): is a zoonotic disease transmitted by both the American dog tick and the RMSF tick, and in order for the disease to be transmitted, the tick must be attached to the dog's skin for a minimum of five hours.

Common symptoms are many and may include fever, reduced appetite, depression, painful joints, lameness, vomiting and diarrhoea, and some dogs may develop pneumonia, heart abnormalities, liver damage, kidney failure, or even neurological signs, such as seizures or unsteady, wobbly or stumbling gait. A 2-3 week course of antibiotics (Doxycycline or Tetracycline) would be the recommended treatment.

Ehrlichiosis: is a tick-borne disease transmitted by both the brown dog tick and the Lone Star Tick, with common symptoms including reduced appetite, depression, fever, bruising and stiff and painful joints. The signs of infection typically occur less than a month after a tick bite and may last for approximately four weeks. There is no vaccine available and treatment involves a lengthy course of antibiotics.

Anaplasmosis: deer ticks **(pictured)** and Western blacklegged ticks are carriers of the bacteria that transmit canine Anaplasmosis. However, there is also another form of Anaplasmosis (caused by a different bacteria) that is carried by the brown dog tick.

Since the deer tick also carries other diseases, some animals may be at risk of developing more than one tick-borne disease at the same time. Signs are similar to Ehrlichiosis and include painful joints, diarrhoea, fever, and vomiting, and there can also be possible disorders of the nervous system. Treatment involves receiving a 30-day dosage of the antibiotic Doxycycline.

Tick Paralysis (pictured): this zoonotic infection is caused when ticks attach themselves to the skin of a dog and secrete a neurotoxin that compromises the nervous system. Dogs that have been infected usually display weakness and limpness approximately one week after first being bitten.

Recognizable symptoms often begin with a change in pitch of the dog's usual bark, and weakness in the rear legs that eventually involves all four legs, followed by the dog having difficulty breathing and swallowing. Your dog can die if not diagnosed and the tick is properly removed.

Canine Coronavirus: this highly contagious disease of the intestines is spread through contact with the feces of contaminated dogs. While considered a worldwide health problem, this virus can be destroyed by most common, readily available disinfectants. Symptoms include diarrhoea, vomiting and weight loss or anorexia. There is a vaccine available, which is usually given to puppies, because they are more susceptible at a young age. Show dogs may also be vaccinated, because being in close proximity to many other dogs means that they are at a higher risk of being exposed to the disease.

Leptospirosis: is a zoonotic bacterial infection that is found worldwide, and can affect humans and many different kinds of animals, including dogs. If left untreated, there is potential for both dogs and humans to die from this disease.

The good news is that the virus is usually effectively treated with antibiotics and supportive care, and because you can protect your dog with a vaccination, if you reside in an area considered a hot spot for leptospirosis, it makes sense to vaccinate your dog against this disease.

Be Aware: Allergies Can Adversely Affect Your Dog's Health

You may be surprised to learn that our dogs may suffer from allergies in much the same way that people can. Not only can the Labradoodle develop allergies to certain foods, but he or she can also develop inhalant or contact allergies. The general signs of allergic reactions may include the following:

- 🐾 Itchy red skin (**see picture below**)

- 🐾 Itchy or runny eyes

- 🐾 Licking the base of the tail

- 🐾 Sneezing or coughing

- 🐾 Ear infections

- 🐾 Diarrhea

- 🐾 Snoring from throat inflammation

- 🐾 Chewing and licking the paws

A dog can be allergic to many common substances easily found in the environment, including grass, weeds, pollen, mould spores, dust, dander, feathers, cigarette smoke, prescription drugs, perfumes, garden fertilizers and cleaning products.

Your dog can also be allergic to certain flea and tick products, so be very careful which one you choose. You should also never use products on your dog that are not designed specifically for dogs – this includes shampoo and conditioner.

One of the most common complaints discussed at the veterinarian's office when they see dogs obsessively scratching, biting, licking and chewing at their skin or paws is possible allergies, and there can be many triggers. Educating yourself can help to ensure your dog never has to suffer from allergies and can lead a happier, itch-free life.

Environmental allergies: what many of us humans seem to forget is that our dogs can develop allergies to simple things that we might not notice, such as chemicals, car exhaust, dust, grass, mould, pollen, various forms of smoke, or flea and tick preparations. Further, they may be allergic to certain materials such as cotton or wool, or chemicals found in washing soap or in

cleaning products you use around your home.

Visual symptoms of an allergy are usually first noticed on the dog's stomach, inside of their legs, and at their tail or paws. Because many allergies can be seasonal, our dogs will often be more affected in the spring or fall, with some airborne irritants inhaled by your dog resulting in coughing, sneezing or watery eyes.

If your dog seems to be itching or scratching for no apparent reason, and you think they may have come in contact with an irritant found somewhere in your environment, first give them a cleansing bath, with the proper canine shampoo and conditioner to see if this solves the problem.

Junk food allergies: *"True"* food allergies usually account for only about 10% of allergy problems commonly found in our canine friends.

Be aware that itching, chewing and chronic ear infections are not usually caused by food allergies, but rather are the result of a suppressed or compromised immune system, which could be caused by feeding your dog a low-quality diet. Food sensitivity issues can often be resolved completely simply by changing to a higher-quality food that is more easily digested by your fur friend.

For instance, check food ingredients on the label because far too many dog foods contain gluten products that are common allergens to our fur friends. These include ingredients such as corn, wheat and soybeans. Become a savvy label reader and ask questions, before you choose your dog's food.

Take the Time to Learn a Little Canine CPR

Of course, nobody wants to find his or herself in a situation where the life of their precious canine companion is threatened. However, the reality is that accidents sometimes happen. Therefore, educating yourself about how to help save your beloved furry friend (or maybe even someone else's) is valuable time well spent.

First of all, remember to handle an injured dog very carefully and gently. A dog that is traumatized, fearful or in pain, even one that is usually gentle, may lash out and try to bite (use gloves).

Consider taking a class, because there are many animal CPR courses being offered these days through community educational systems or even online.

It's also a good idea to put together a canine first aid kit, both at home and in your vehicle, in case of emergencies, that includes the following items:

- 🐾 Antiseptic Wash for wounds (hydrogen peroxide)

- 🐾 Blanket

- 🐾 Gauze Bandaging

- 🐾 Kwik Stop styptic powder

- 🐾 Medical Tape

- 🐾 Nail Clippers

- 🐾 Non-Stick Bandages for wounds

- 🐾 Scissors

- 🐾 Sterile Eye Wash

- 🐾 Tick Twister

- 🐾 Towel

- 🐾 Tweezers

- 🐾 Wash cloth

- 🐾 Gloves (in case the dog is trying to bite)

It would also be prudent to obtain a copy of the American Red Cross emergency techniques, called *"Saving Your Pet With CPR"* (at the end of this Chapter), and learn about the proper way to administer CPR to a dog.

Artificial Respiration Step by Step

If your dog becomes unconscious, depending upon what happened to them, they may stop breathing and if they stop breathing, they will go into cardiac arrest, when the heart stops beating and the dog may soon die.

However, after breathing stops, and before cardiac arrest, the heart can continue to beat for several minutes. This is a window of opportunity for performing cardiopulmonary resuscitation (CPR) or artificial respiration, which can save your dog's life.

Step 1: place your dog on their right side on a flat surface.

Step 2: check to make sure that your dog has actually stopped breathing by watching for the rise and fall of their chest and feel for their breath on your hand. Check the colour of your dog's gums, because lack of oxygen will make them turn blue.

Step 3: check that the dog's airway is clear and there is nothing stuck in their mouth or throat by extending the head and neck and opening your dog's mouth.

If there is an object blocking their throat, pull the tongue outward and use your fingers or tweezers to get a firm grip on the object so that you can pull it free from the dog's throat. If you cannot reach the object that appears to be blocking the dog's airway passage, you will have to use the Heimlich Manoeuvre to try and dislodge it (see next section).

Step 4: so long as the dog's airway is not blocked, you can lift their chin to straighten out the neck and begin rescue breathing.

Step 5: hold the dog's muzzle, close their mouth, put your mouth over the dog's nose and blow gently – just enough to cause the dog's chest to rise.

Step 6: wait long enough for the air you just breathed into the dog's lungs to leave before giving another breath.

Step 7: continue giving one gentle breath every 3 seconds as long as the heart is still beating or until your dog starts to breathe on their own.

Canine Heimlich Manoeuvre

If breath won't go in, the airway may be blocked. In this case, you will need to turn your dog upside down, with his or her back held against your chest.

Wrap your arms around the dog and clasp your hands together just below the dog's rib cage (since the dog is being held upside down, this will actually be above the rib cage, in the abdomen).

Using both arms, give five sharp thrusts to the abdomen, and then check the dog's mouth or airway for the object. If the object is visible, remove it, and give two more rescue breaths.

CPR Step by Step

If your dog's heart has stopped beating, then CPR must be started immediately. In an ideal situation, one person could perform the artificial respiration, while the other performs the CPR.

Step 1: put your dog on his or her right side on a flat surface.

Step 2: feel for your dog's pulse or heartbeat by placing one hand over his or her left side, just behind the front leg.

Step 3: place the palm of your hand on your dog's rib cage over his or her heart, with your other hand on top of the first (for puppies, put just your thumb on one side of the chest and the rest of your fingers on the other side).

Step 4: press down and release, compressing the dog's chest approximately one inch (2-3 centimetres) and squeeze and release 80 to 100 times every minute.

While it's always the hope that you may never need to, if your dog is not breathing and there is no pulse, knowing what steps to take in an emergency (which includes how to do the doggy Heimlich Manoeuvre or apply compressions), could literally save the life of your own beloved dog or maybe even someone else's.

In a Nutshell

While your dog will hopefully never have to suffer from any of the common diseases, viruses or health problems that have been statistically known to affect the breed parents of the Labradoodle hybrid, you will probably still want to know what *may* afflict your dog because being aware of the signs associated with certain health issues can help him or her live a longer life.

As well, becoming familiar with emergency CPR procedures outlined in the following American Red Cross chart could help you save your dog's life.

It may also be a good idea to take the time to choose a veterinarian that specializes in the care of small animals for yearly health check-ups, have your dog spayed or neutered in a timely fashion and educate yourself about required vaccinations and how often boosters really need to be administered.

Taking the steps outlined in this Chapter will help ensure that your dog will always have the best opportunity to be healthy and happy throughout your lifelong journey together.

Saving your pet with CPR

With pets increasingly being treated like a member of the family, many owners are learning emergency techniques like CPR to keep their pet alive before bringing it to a veterinarian.

If there is no breathing and no pulse, begin CPR immediately.

Areas to check for pulse

Check for breathing and pulse

Check pulse using middle and index finger below the wrist, inner thigh (femoral artery), below the ankle or where left elbow touches the chest.

Look for other warning signs

· Gums and lips will appear gray- colored.
· Pupils will be dilated and not responsive to light.

Gums

Pupils

If not breathing, give breath to animal

Cats and small dogs
Place your mouth over its nose and mouth to blow air in.

Medium–large dogs
Place your mouth over its nose to blow air in.

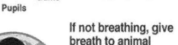

Heimlich maneuver

If breath won't go in, airway may be blocked. Turn dog upside down, with its back against your chest. Wrap your arms around the dog and clasp your hands together just below its rib cage (since you're holding the dog upside down, it's above the rib cage, in the abdomen). Using both arms, give five sharp thrusts to the abdomen. Then check its mouth or airway for the object. If you see it, remove it and give two more rescue breaths.

Start compressions if no pulse

Lay animal on right side and place hand over ribs where its elbow touches the chest. Begin compressions. Do not give compressions if dog has pulse.

Animal size	Compress chest	Compressions per breath of air
Cat/small dog (Under 30 lbs.)	1/2-1 inch	5
Medium–large dog (30–90 lbs.)	1–3 inches	5
Giant dog (over 90 lbs.)	1–3 inches	10

Repeat procedure
· Check pulse after 1 minute and then every few minutes.
· Continue giving CPR until the animal has a pulse and is breathing.
· Stop CPR after 20 minutes.

SOURCE: American Red Cross

Chapter 5: Let Your Dog BE a Happy Dog

*"Don't make the mistake of treating your dogs
like humans, or they'll treat you like dogs."*
— Martha Scott

This chapter is written to give you a heads up about the fact that WE humans can actually be the cause of future problems. This is because far too many of us humans have the tendency to treat our dogs more like human fur children than dogs.

It's important to understand that not allowing your fur friend to be *"dog-like"* when we're talking about THEIR happiness can be a problem, because treating a dog like a human can ultimately result in the dog's humans creating any number of unwanted behavioural issues.

Your Dog is Not a Child

While this might sound like a strange thing to say, there is no doubt that many humans simply don't allow their dogs to actually BE dogs, because they are too busy confusing their dog by allowing them to be the boss, attributing human emotions to them, and treating them more like children.

Today, the urge for humans to treat their dogs much more like children than dogs is becoming an ever-increasing serious problem, and perhaps contributing to this phenomenon is the fact that many Millennials and single people are choosing to have dogs instead of children.

The reality is that no matter the size or breed of the dog, if you want them to be happy, they still need to be accepted as dogs and they need their humans to have strong enough energy to lead them. When humans begin to expect their dog to fulfill an emotional void that can only be met by another human, we may soon find ourselves travelling down a road that can lead to many problems for both human and dog.

Yes, some dogs may need to wear clothing to provide protection from the cold and rain during the winter months. However, if the only reason you are dressing up your dog and treating them like a human child is because it makes you laugh, or appeals to a frustrated parental instinct, this may be a less than healthy relationship.

 With respect to canine clothing, if you live in a warm climate, you may want to provide your dog (especially one with a darker coat) with a cooling vest or a simple white t-shirt to reflect the heat during warmer summer months when they are walking outside in the sunshine because this can keep them considerably cooler.

When your dog is a full-grown adult, you will definitely want to begin more complicated or advanced training sessions. They will enjoy the attention and time spent with you and when you have the desire and patience, this dog is very willing to please, which means that there is literally no end to what you can teach this very smart, energetic, and eager to learn dog.

While some breeds of dogs of lower intelligence might be perfectly fine without receiving daily interesting activities to keep them busy and mentally challenged, the Labradoodle likes to solve problems; with their high intelligence and curious and playful temperament, they typically want and need to occupy much more of their guardian's time and energy by engaging in physical activities that also challenge them mentally.

A conscientious guardian of this breed will need to constantly be thinking of interesting ways to challenge their alert and inquisitive canine companion to make this dog's daily life interesting.

If you and your dog are really enjoying learning new routines and tricks together, you might want to advance to teaching them the hand signals for more complicated tricks, such as *"commando crawl"*, how to *"speak"* or to *"jump through the human hoop"*, and depending on your particular dog, you may want to consider getting them involved in a fun canine sport, like Agility, Flyball, Barn Hunt, Advanced Obedience or even get them certified as a therapy dog.

 The only restriction to how far you can go with training your dog will be your time and imagination and their personal energy level, ability and desire to perform.

Every one of our chosen canine companions has a uniquely wonderful set of gifts and talents to share with their human counterparts, if only us humans would listen. They *"tell"* us when they are unhappy, frightened, bored, nervous, and when they are under-exercised, yet often we're not paying attention because we're caught up in the business of our human world, or we think they are just being badly behaved.

If you are deciding to have dogs instead of children, be careful that you don't get caught up in attempting to manipulate your dog into being a furry child. Trying to turn a dog into a fur-covered human has had a seriously detrimental effect upon the health, happiness and behaviour of so many of our canine companions.

Single, lonely people often have dogs, which is perfectly fine, so long as the human side of the equation doesn't expect their canine counterpart to fulfill what humans require on an emotional level, because this can be very confusing to a dog who needs their human to lead them.

 The Labradoodle is not a breed well suited for the physically restricted or inactive individual or for humans that lead busy lives with long work schedules that keep them away from home. In order

for this smart, sensitive and loving dog to be well balanced psychologically, they demand a lot of attention and will not be happy spending only a few minutes with their humans each day.

This dog will also not be very happy leading a sedentary life because they have endless stamina and are highly energetic, curious and interested in what's going on around them. They need to get out and about on a regular basis, rather than simply lazing about all day.

In order to be the best guardians for our four-legged friends, and have a more harmonious relationship, we humans must have a better understanding of what our dogs need from us, rather than what we need from them. This way, our chosen canine companions can live in safety, harmony and security within our human environment.

Sadly, many owners are not well equipped to give their dogs what they really need, or they don't have the right energy for the dog they choose, which is what leads to so many homeless, abandoned and frustrated, out of control dogs and so many overflowing rescue facilities.

 As a professional dog whisperer who is regularly challenged with the task of finding amicable solutions for canine/human relationships that have become unbalanced, I can tell you with absolute certainty that once humans understand what needs to be changed and are willing to take the steps to do the work required, almost every stressful canine/human relationship can be turned into a happy one.

The sad part is that many humans are simply not aware of how important it is to really understand their own energy and capabilities, and whether they are compatible with the breed they are choosing. Further, sometimes humans forget to factor in how much time they really have to do the consistent work required on a daily basis in order to meet their chosen dog's needs. Getting a dog will drastically change your life.

Almost ALL canine problems, both mentally and physically, are a direct result of incompatible energy and lifestyle between dog and human.

Choosing a dog without first seriously researching the breed and then being honest about your own lifestyle and how much time you can truly devote to a dog, will almost certainly cause problems to arise somewhere down the road.

It's no secret that lack of knowledge and experience, not acknowledging realistic time restraints or forgetting about taking a good look at our human lifestyle can be a typical human mistake when choosing the right dog.

It's also no secret that if these important factors are not taken into consideration, learning about what a dog truly needs and being able to provide it will be a hit and miss undertaking that may often result in the "miss" coming out on top.

What we humans often forget to consider is that first and foremost, our dogs need to be respected for their unique canine qualities and capabilities and we need to recognize and fully appreciate how willing they are to bend themselves to our will so that they can fit into our human environment.

For millennia, dog has been considered *"Man's best friend"*. In today's society, when we want to do the best for our canine companions and create a happy, mutually beneficial relationship, we humans need to spend more time receiving the proper training WE need, so that we can learn how to be *"Dog's best friend"*.

Any dog can be a *"best friend"* to a human, providing that we humans educate ourselves, choose wisely and put in the work. This is a universal truth that applies to any canine breed, including the active, affectionate and highly intelligent Labradoodle.

PERSONAL EXPERIENCE: Many times, I've been asked to come and correct "problems" in a family that has decided to share their lives with an energetic Labradoodle. For instance, they are embarrassed because they cannot leave the house without their dog howling or barking and disturbing the neighbors. They often show me pictures of an excavated back yard or chewed coffee table legs and expect me to "fix" their unruly dog

In every instance, the dog is being blamed for not wanting to spend hours alone, being under-exercised, improperly socialised and never having been taught rules and boundaries. Even worse is when a dog in this situation has also been forced to be the boss of their surroundings because the human guardian in the relationship has very soft energy that the dog cannot trust, respect or follow. None of this is the dog's fault, and there's a lot of work to be done here before this type of situation can be positively turned around.

While the dog is eagerly willing to change right away when they get what they need, for us humans it's usually a much longer road to break us out of our predictable routines and learn new ways that will set this type of situation right. Unfortunately, many of us simply don't have what it takes, don't have the time to do the work, are not willing to change, or are not comfortable with admitting that we may have caused the problem in the first place. What follows can often be another dog abandoned and placed behind bars at the local SPCA.

Choose wisely and please don't let this ever be your story.

For anyone considering this smart, energetic dog for your family, be absolutely certain that you are aware of their past history, and that you are able to involve him or her in interesting vigorous daily routines and tasks that will engage both body and mind. Also, be sure that you have strong enough energy and can teach the firm rules and boundaries that this dog needs to trust, respect and follow you.

Providing firm guidance for this energetic, tireless, and robust dog will ensure that you are raising a happy dog that never has to suffer from the stress of behavioural issues that can lead to poor health.

In a Nutshell

It's important to understand that no matter the size or breed of your chosen canine friend, you actually need to find appropriate ways to let your dog BE a dog if you want to raise a happy and healthy companion.

While being overly protective, babying them or treating them like a fur-covered child may be something YOU need, it's not what THEY need.

If you are not able to consistently participate in being a strong role model that takes on the leadership role for the Labradoodle, he or she may become confused about who is the boss. Be aware that confusion about who is the alpha dog in this relationship has the potential to result in the creation of unwanted behavioural issues sooner or later in life.

Chapter 6: Every Happy Labradoodle Wants Exercise

*"The dog lives for the day,
the hour, even the moment."*
— Robert Scott

This breed will usually require a moderate to high amount of vigorous daily physical and mental exercise, that also includes going out for 2-3 on-leash walks, walking properly at your side (without pulling) every day.

The very smart Labradoodle will also need space to run (or swim) freely and some challenging thinking tasks that exercise the brain. A varied and interesting daily routine will result in a strong bond of trust and respect between you and your dog that translates to both a healthy body and a healthy mind.

If you are unable to commit to the time required to ensure your dog receives regular exercise each day, that engages both mind and body, this will soon be a very bored, overweight, unhappy, stressed dog that could develop multiple health and behaviour issues.

Minimum Daily Exercise Requirements

A minimum of three 30 to 60 minute, on-leash, disciplined walks outdoors every day where they are walking calmly at your side without pulling, while also paying close attention to your commands.

A minimum of one hour running, swimming, hiking, romping and socialising with other dogs or performing an interesting canine sport, plus 15 to 30 minutes every day teaching tricks, commands, hand signals or routines that will exercise the brain.

Once properly leash trained and heeding basic commands, the Labradoodle will also need the reward of some off-leash freedom at a securely fenced local dog park where (under your close supervision) they can run, socialise, play with other dogs or perhaps fetch a ball or Frisbee and just enjoy being a dog.

When playing a game of fetch, be careful that you do not teach your dog to swear at you or be disrespectful. You've seen it yourself I'm sure, or at least heard it. This is when a dog has been taught by their humans to be ball or Frisbee obsessed. When the dog and human arrive at the park you can already hear the dog barking at their human to throw the ball before they're even out of the vehicle.

PERSONAL EXPERIENCE: *I've had first hand experience that demonstrates just how quickly a ball-obsessed dog can take over the game. My husband and I took a young Australian terrier, who loved to chase fast-moving objects, to our local park, and we decided to take a ball so that the dog could really run. Unfortunately, my husband put the ball in his coat pocket and when we arrived at the park, he immediately threw it for the terrier, before taking the time to have the dog sit, make eye contact, and patiently wait. Now, every time this dog sees my husband, if he has a hand in his coat pocket, the dog immediately starts to bark, thinking if he barks, a ball will appear that he will get to chase.*

Don't Let the Dog Be in Charge

If you don't take the time to curb a barking habit during play, or at other inappropriate times, you may have to endure a noisy problem that will be irritating to you and everyone else within earshot for the life of your dog.

The Labradoodle will usually love to chase a fast-moving ball or Frisbee, and when playing a game of fetch, it may take only seconds for this clever canine to teach their humans that they are in charge of the game. Literally, if you are not aware of what you are "teaching", all it may take is one slip up. Once you've made this mistake, your smart dog may never forget that when the ball comes out, they are in charge, which means that correcting this irritating habit may take a very long time.

Consider that your dog is excited to retrieve the ball or Frisbee, so he or she barks, and you immediately throw the desired object. Guess what? You just taught your dog to bark (or swear) at you to immediately get what they want.

To do nothing about your dog barking for what they want sends an unspoken message to him or her that you approve of this type of bossy behaviour. If you simply laugh, thinking this is such a funny scene, you will be teaching your dog to continue to swear at you. Don't go there in the first place, because reversing this noisy problem can take many long and frustrating hours to accomplish.

Instead, teach patience, be a proactive leader for your dog and help him or her learn what is, and what is not acceptable. When you draw a firm line in the sand and are always consistent with enforcing rules and boundaries, there will be no confusion, and you will have given your loyal companion the best opportunity for a happy and stress-free life. Teach your dog to slow it down, be patient and make eye contact with YOU (not the ball or Frisbee) before you throw it.

The smart Labradoodle can sometimes be stubborn because they come from a working background and are used to thinking for his or herself. This makes it even more important to always be firmly consistent when teaching and enforcing rules and boundaries.

Your dog needs to know that YOU are always in control of what they do, whether playing a game or interacting with other dogs, and that you will never permit any overly boisterous activity with other dogs or any attempt to dominate, be aggressive or chase other animals without your say so.

Keeping your dog "safe" first means teaching them rules and boundaries and then always being consistent and vigilant about enforcing them. While the Labradoodle is usually friendly with unknown dogs, if you are uncertain about another dog approaching, simply place yourself between your dog and the approaching dog until you're certain a friendly greeting will be the outcome.

Ideal Daily Exercise Requirements

A fully-grown Labradoodle will be a playful, energetic and versatile dog with endless stamina that will excel when they receive a wide variety of fun and interesting daily mental and physical stimulation. This should include disciplined walks, exercise, play and challenging mental games or canine sports.

Always tireless and eager for their next adventure at the side of their human guardian, depending on what you have the desire to teach, this dog's skills can be many.

Keep in mind that, depending on the particular dog and how you raise him or her, they will generally be more or less energetic. It's a simple formula: you are more energetic, your dog is more energetic and both of you will be healthier and happier.

I've known Labradoodle clients whose dogs were bored, frustrated, under-exercised and overweight, and others whose dogs were amazing athletes whose days were filled with energetic outdoor pursuits that kept both mind and body fit and healthy. In other words, if you're active, your dog most likely will be too.

There may be many sports and services that could be appropriate for this strong, versatile, super smart and energetic dog that include, but are not limited to:

🐾 Advanced Obedience

- 🐾 Agility

- 🐾 Flyball

- 🐾 Disc Dog

- 🐾 Dock Diving

- 🐾 Barn Hunt

- 🐾 Rally Trials

- 🐾 Trick Training

- 🐾 Therapy or Service

This friendly dog has great stamina and loves to run and retrieve fast-moving objects. Another very good way to give them the amount of exercise they really need is to train them to jog beside your bicycle. Consider training this energetic dog to a *"Springer Bicycle Jogger"* **(pictured)**, so that they can receive a good amount of disciplined, vigorous exercise in a short period of time. Make sure you don't pedal too  fast, never overdo it, and always carry water for your dog.

The *"Springer Bicycle Jogger"* attachment for a bicycle is an ideal and safe way to adequately exercise this dog, while still keeping them under proper control, so that they cannot chase after a bird, cat or other distraction.

The Springer easily attaches to any bicycle and the arm can be quickly removed when not needed. The large spring attaches to a harness on the dog and there is a quick release, break-away tab at the top of the rope in case the dog runs around one side of a pole while you and the bike are on the other side. As well, the large spring in this arrangement ensures that if your dog tries to lunge or chase a squirrel or other distraction, you and your bicycle will remain upright.

Depending of the size and weight of your Labradoodle, if your dog is larger and very strong, another form of exercise, that can be great fun for both dog and human alike, is the *"Dog Powered Scooter"* (look it up online), where the dog is attached by harness to a scooter so that the dog is the power for the human riding the scooter.

Ideal Living Conditions for a Happy Labradoodle

This fun-loving companion needs a vigorous daily schedule that includes getting outside for their disciplined, on-leash walks, socialising, and participating in interesting tasks where they get to use their brain, plus the opportunity to freely run every day.

Also, keep in mind that the personality of every dog will be different and depending on their human leadership, your dog will develop traits, quirks and talents that are unique to him or her.

How each puppy will develop will depend upon careful and conscientious breeding, temperament of the parents, the environment where they are raised and how they are trained and socialised.

The intelligent, eager to learn and easy to train Labradoodle will do best with a consistently fair yet firm guardian that maintains rules and boundaries that they can respect, and he or she will respond well to training programs involving treat-based rewards or reinforcement.

"First, I want you to make sure that my dog is still in there someplace."

Properly socialising at a young age, during the first three months of his or her life, will greatly influence this dog's adult temperament, personality and behaviour as he or she matures, and will help to prevent this dog from becoming shy or nervous.

Continuing to shape the personality of this dog through adolescence and on into adulthood with a combination of socialising, training, plenty of exercise, and consistent rules and boundaries, will help to ensure a trustworthy, friendly and well-mannered fur friend.

If you are unable to commit to providing an appropriate routine for this energetic dog on a daily basis, that includes mental games, and spending as much time as possible engaged in vigorous outdoor pursuits each day, this strong and athletic dog will very likely become unhealthily overweight. As well, beyond becoming depressed or frustrated, without adequate mental and physical exercise and proper socialising, this dog may become overly wary around other dogs, which can lead to nervous aggression.

An under-exercised dog will soon become fat, bored and unhappy, which can then cause them to develop unwanted problems that could include acting out in destructive ways by chewing "off limits" items in the home, digging holes in the garden, escaping the back yard, excessive barking, and ultimately suffering from anxiety and stress that can prematurely affect their health and shorten their life.

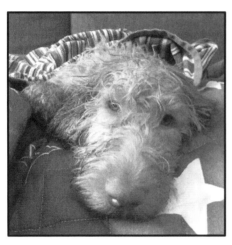

Above all else, never forget that all dogs (no matter their size) are pack animals, which means that it is not normal for them to spend long periods of time in lonely isolation. It's even more important that a highly energetic, smart and often sensitive dog that comes from a working background, such as the Labradoodle, has consistent contact with their humans, and plenty of interesting tasks to keep them occupied.

Always remember that when you adopt a dog into your family you become their pack and you cannot simply abandon them, forget about their needs, and leave them to their own devices when it's convenient for you to do so.

In other words, if you're planning to leave your dog alone for many hours every day, while you're at work or out for an evening at the pub with friends, perhaps you're not yet ready for the big change in lifestyle that comes hand in hand with being the ideal dog guardian.

Dogs that are left alone too much often develop separation anxiety, a depressed and unhappy state of mind, destructive tendencies and angry neighbours should your dog spend his or her lonely hours barking up a storm.

In a Nutshell

The bottom line here is that the Labradoodle is a strong, athletic, very smart, and affectionate dog that likes to keep busy while in the close company of their humans. This dog has endless stamina and NEEDS a consistent leader and plenty of interesting and fun activity to keep them happy and contented every day.

Even before you bring this adorable puppy home, start thinking about your ability to be a good leader, the importance of early and on-going socialisation, firm training and consistent enforcement of rules and boundaries.

Once you've got all of this in hand, then it will be time to consider involving this brilliant dog in Advanced Obedience, Trick Training, Barn Hunt, Flyball, Agility, Dock Diving and many other canine sports, that should be in the future for this highly capable fur friend.

This Chapter suggests many different canine sports that this versatile dog may naturally excel at. Truly consider involving him or her in a sport, because this is a great way to provide them with the exercise they need in a disciplined way that will engage their mind while keeping them slim and trim.

Teaching an activity or sporting routine will help to establish a firm bond of trust and respect between you, and ensure that your dog is a healthy and happy family member, while also teaching them that you have what it takes to lead them, so that they will always follow without question.

Chapter 7: Feeding the Happy Labradoodle

"I feel sorry for people who don't have dogs.
I hear they have to pick up food they drop on the floor."
— Unknown

A properly fed dog means a healthy, happy and longer-lived companion, so make sure that you dedicate some time to researching high-quality food and treats that will be the most appropriate for your canine athlete, and don't overfeed.

DID YOU KNOW? *This dog may be strongly food motivated. If there is food around, they may not know when to stop, so be careful not to overfeed or leave food items within their reach.*

We are what we eat, and the same is absolutely true for our canine companions. The Labradoodle is a combination of two breeds that are usually highly food motivated.

Make sure that you don't get into the habit of *"doctoring"* their food bowl with your human food. If you do, a dog that may be less food motivated than others may soon refuse to eat their doggy dinner. Don't worry, though, because even a picky eater (which is highly unlikely with this breed) will not starve him or herself, and if they refuse their expensive dog dinner tonight, so long as you don't cave, they WILL be hungry tomorrow.

First, remember that our canine friends are carnivores, which means that they derive their energy and nutrient requirements that will maintain their health by consuming a diet consisting mainly or exclusively of the flesh of animal tissues. In other words, your dog is a meat eater.

Many dog people are unaware of the importance of feeding their dog a high-quality dog food and may often make the mistake of shopping for dog food by price or convenience alone. The problem with this method is that in most cases, the cheaper the dog food is, the lower quality and less nutritious it will be.

Inexpensive dog food brands contain cheap, inferior fillers (corn, soy and wheat) and other unnecessary ingredients to add bulk to the product, rather than providing any nutritional benefit. Without a healthy, high-quality, balanced diet, your dog may not live as long as he or she could because poorly chosen food may often lead to the development of health problems.

When choosing an appropriate diet for your Labradoodle, first considering the physiology of the canine's teeth, jaws and digestive tract may help provide you with a better insight into what type of food your dog should be eating.

Teeth, Jaws, and Digestive Tract

Teeth: canine teeth are all sharp and pointed because they are designed to rip, shred and tear into animal meat and crush bone. An adult dog has on average a third more teeth than his or her human guardian.

Adult canines have 42 permanent teeth in comparison to our measly 32 human teeth (without counting any wisdom teeth, which are a "bonus"). On average, puppies have 28 baby teeth, while human babies will possess 20 "baby" teeth. Puppies begin to lose those sharp baby teeth at approximately 12 to 16 weeks of age. By four months of age, almost all of a puppy's milk teeth will have been shed and replaced by the strong, permanent adult teeth.

Jaws: every dog is born equipped with powerful jaws and neck muscles for the specific purpose of being able to pull down and tear apart their hunted prey.

The jaw of every canine can open widely to hold large pieces of meat and bone, while the actual mechanics of the jaw permits only vertical (up and down) movement that is designed for crushing.

Digestive Tract: the canine digestive tract is short, simple and designed to move their natural choice of food (hide, meat and bone) quickly through their systems.

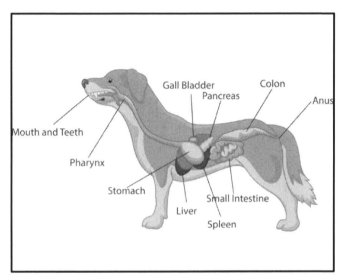

We humans need vegetables and plant matter in our diet to stay healthy and have the flat molars to effectively crush and chew them. While we often believe our dogs require the same, when choosing an appropriate food source for your Labradoodle, you need to consider that vegetables and plant matter require much more time to break down in the gastrointestinal tract. This in turn, requires a more complex digestive system that the canine body simply does not have.

For instance, the dog's digestive system is unable to effectively break down vegetable matter, which is why whole vegetables look pretty much the same going into your dog, as they do coming out the other end.

Consider how much healthier and longer-lived your beloved dog might be if, rather than largely ignoring nature's design for our canine companions, instead we chose to feed them whole, unprocessed, species-appropriate food.

Whatever you decide to feed your dog, consider that just as too much wheat or other grains and fillers in our human diet are having detrimental effects on our human health, the same can be very true for our dogs.

Get into the habit of carefully reading labels so that you can be certain to avoid unbalanced foods that contain unwanted fillers or high amounts of grains, because these are not part of a healthy canine diet.

Also consider that even though dogs ARE carnivores, some do very well on a "plant based" diet simply because so many of our meat sources are polluted with wheat, chemicals, hormones, drugs and other products that would not be part of a wild dog's natural diet.

As an example, one of the world's longest living canines was a highly energetic Border Collie who was fed a clean plant-based diet, and lived to be over 25 years of age, even though average for this breed is 14.

Control of Your Happy Labradoodle's Food

While some dogs may be picky eaters, and some may have a moderately healthy appetite, others can be so voracious at feeding time that you wonder if they're going to eat the bowl, too. The robust and energetic Labradoodle most likely falls into the "voracious" category (like both of their parents), and because they are deep chested, if they wolf down their food, they can suffer from life-threatening bloat. *You will most likely want to get this dog a slow feeder type of bowl to slow them down.*

Any dog can get bored with eating the same food every day, and if yours does, it won't hurt to mix it up a little. For instance, my dog, Boris, usually had little interest in food during the morning, but was always ready for his dental treat at high noon. His internal clock was spot on and if I was not keeping an eye on the clock, he would just calmly sit there staring at me until I got it.

It's important that your dog understands that YOU are in control of their food source. Once they understand this, they will also figure out that there will be windows of opportunity for receiving and eating their food, and this type of routine will help to develop healthy eating habits.

Many people use a scoop or measuring cup to put dry food into their dog's bowl. Why this may be a mistake is because it's very important to mix your dog's food with your hands, so that your scent is all over the food, before you offer it to them to eat. This sends a subliminal "message" to your dog that you are their pack leader, because it mimics what would happen if you were the alpha dog out hunting with the pack for your food in the wild.

For instance, while a pack of wild dogs hunting for food all work hard to capture their prey, the alpha pack leader always gets to eat first while all the other dogs must patiently wait until the leader of the pack eats their fill and moves away, before they can rush in to eat what is left over.

Therefore, when you mix your domesticated dog's dinner with your hands, you will be sending them the subtle message that YOU are their pack leader, you've already eaten your fill and are now allowing them to eat what is left over.

Nutritional Needs of the Labradoodle

Another crime that only CSI could solve.

Before you go dog food shopping, take the time to learn the basics about the nutritional needs of your particular fur friend. Dogs are primarily carnivorous animals, which means that most of their nutritional needs should come from animal sources, such as meat, fish, and eggs.

Your dog requires a balance of protein and fat in their diet, plus healthy carbohydrates that can provide energy, fibre and other essential nutrients. It's important that your dog's daily food intake provides for their basic nutritional needs, because this is what he or she will be eating throughout most of their life.

If you want to get into the specifics, know that protein is the most important nutrient for a dog and is required for healthy puppy growth and development. When your puppy grows up, protein will help him or her maintain lean muscle mass, so they do not become overweight or obese.

While your puppy needs at least 22% protein in their diet during the growing stage, an adult dog needs 18%.

Next to protein, the most important nutrient for dogs is fat. While you may think of fat as a bad thing, it's actually an essential part of a balanced diet for dogs. Fat provides a concentrated source of energy and it helps your dog absorb and utilize fat-soluble vitamins. Fat should come from healthy animal sources such as chicken fat or salmon oil and should make up at least 8% of a growing dog's diet. An adult dog will require a minimum of 5%.

Technically speaking, while dogs do not have specific requirements for carbohydrate in their diet, carbs can provide energy as well as fibre and other nutrients.

What you also need to remember is that your dog's body is not optimized for digesting and absorbing nutrition from plant products as much as from animal products, which means that carbohydrates in your dog's diet should be limited. Any carbohydrates in a dog's diet should also come from easily digestible sources, such as beans or legumes, starchy vegetables (sweet potatoes, pumpkin, squash) and whole grains.

Choosing a High-Quality Dog Food Brand

When food shopping for your dog, take your time and carefully read the information on the bag or box so that you can determine the quality of the food inside.

Also, if you're going to compare different products, remember to keep in mind three specific things to look for on the label.

(1) AAFCO Statement of Nutritional Adequacy

First, look for the Association of American Feed Control Officials (AAFCO) statement of nutritional adequacy. This organization sets and upholds standards for pet and animal feed in the United States. If you and your dog live in the United Kingdom, these standards will be regulated by the Food Standards Agency (FSA).

Before a product makes its way to the consumer's shelf, these types of organizations examine the product to make sure it meets the minimum nutritional requirements for the intended animal, which, in this case, is your dog. When the product in question is nutritionally balanced for dogs, you will see a statement like this somewhere on the label:

"[Product Name] is formulated to meet the nutritional levels established by the AAFCO Dog Food Nutrient Profiles."

If this is written on the package, you can rest assured that it has been manufactured to meet your dog's <u>minimum</u> nutritional needs. Keep in mind, however, that the AAFCO statement does not guarantee quality. This means that you still have to actually read the ingredients list noted on the package to determine whether or not the particular product is a nutritious choice for your dog.

(2) Guaranteed Analysis

After the AAFCO statement, check the product for the guaranteed analysis. This will indicate the percentages of protein, fat, fibre and moisture contained in the product. You can use the guaranteed analysis to make a direct comparison between products using those minimum values from the last section. Since dogs digest meat much more efficiently than they do plant foods, you will want to look for products that contain a fibre content that is less than 5%.

(3) Ingredients List

After checking the guaranteed analysis, the final place to look is the ingredients list, which will be noted in descending order by percentage of volume.

This means that the ingredients at the top of the list make up the highest quantity, which is the same for packages of food we humans eat. You will want to see healthy, high-quality ingredients at the top of the list, beginning with a quality source of animal protein. Dogs are carnivores, which means that their bodies are better able to digest and absorb nutrition from animal sources. Quality sources of animal protein for dogs include poultry, meat, and seafood.

Aside from proteins, fats, and carbohydrates, there are other beneficial ingredients to be aware of. Supplemental vitamins and minerals can improve your dog's health, because they help to protect a dog's immune system and ensure that your fur friend's specific nutritional needs are met.

DID YOU KNOW? *Synthetic supplements are not as good for your dog as natural sources for the same nutrients – such as fresh fruits and vegetables. With respect to mineral supplements, chelated minerals are ideal because they have been bound to protein molecules, which make them easier for your dog's body to utilize. If you see "dried fermentation products" added to the list, these are helpful probiotics that can support your dog's digestion.*

Feeding Tips

- Feeding amounts for canines vary based on several factors, such as breed, lifestyle, age, body condition and daily exercise.

- While feeding suggestions are noted on all dog food packaging, your vet may be the best resource for educating you about exactly how much you should be feeding your dog. Refer to the next section for generic guidelines about feeding amounts.

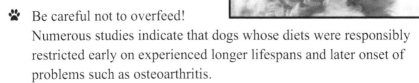

- Consult your vet regularly about your puppy's weight as achieving and maintaining an ideal weight not only reduces many health risks, but can also be instrumental in helping your dog enjoy a more energetic, longer and healthier life.

- Be careful not to overfeed! Numerous studies indicate that dogs whose diets were responsibly restricted early on experienced longer lifespans and later onset of problems such as osteoarthritis.

- If you give your dog the occasional treat or if you use treats for training, always remember to take these additional calories into account and, if necessary, reduce their daily food amount accordingly.

❧ As a rule of thumb, treats shouldn't make up more than 10% of your dog's daily calorie intake, because feeding more can unbalance his or her diet.

❧ Although it's tempting and convenient to feed your puppy human table scraps, human food often does not provide the proper balance of nutrients that a healthy dog requires.

❧ A puppy or adult dog rarely says no to food, and they are always very interested in what their humans are eating. However, that does not mean they are always hungry. Constantly giving your dog food can lead to unwanted behaviour problems, such as "begging for food" and hyper activity whenever they see you eating. Dogs are hard wired to always be foraging and looking for food and no matter how much you feed them, most dogs will still ask for more. Therefore, make sure you don't let your dog develop this bad habit of begging for food.

❧ If you have decided to change your dog's diet, be sure to mix a little of the old food with the new food to transition them slowly over the period of several days because this will help to prevent digestive upsets.

❧ When you mix your dog's food properly and he or she is still experiencing digestive issues, it could be something else – such as food allergies.

❧ Food allergies affect dogs in a different way from how they affect humans. While you might feel nauseous or sick after eating something you are allergic to, your dog will be more likely to develop skin problems, or throw up what they just ate.

❧ Red, itchy, and inflamed skin is a common sign of food allergies.

* Technically, while your dog can develop an allergy to any food he or she eats, there are some common ingredients more likely to trigger food allergies in dogs.

* Some of the most common food allergens for dogs can include beef, chicken, dairy, lamb, fish, corn, eggs, wheat, and soy. The allergic reaction is usually because they came from food sources that are not "clean" or "organic". For instance, to rule out food as an allergen, the chosen food would need to be certified organic, grass fed, and containing no harmful additives, such as hormones or chemicals that are hidden components that can cause allergic responses. Crops such as corn, soy or wheat are often sprayed with chemicals and fed to farmed animals to fatten them up. This means that your dog may not actually be allergic to beef, but may be allergic to the wheat, soy or corn that was sprayed with chemicals that's been fed to the animals.

* If you are worried that your dog is suffering from a food allergy, you may need to put him or her on an elimination diet for 12 weeks or until all signs of the allergy have disappeared. At that point you can either keep feeding the elimination diet or switch to a food that doesn't contain the suspected allergen.

Feeding Puppies

A general rule of thumb for growing Labradoodle puppies is to feed daily amounts of between 2 and 3% of what the puppy's adult weight is projected to be or 10% of the puppy's current body weight. You will want to keep in mind that while all growing puppies

require extra protein to help them develop into healthy adult dogs, this is especially important with muscular, higher energy puppies, like the Labradoodle.

You will also want to keep a close eye to make sure that your puppy is eating and drinking enough throughout the day, so set regular feeding times and stick to them. The smaller the puppy, the more important this will be.

Today there are many foods on the market specifically formulated for all stages of a dog's life (including the puppy stage). Whether you choose one of these foods or a food formulated just for puppies, they will need to be fed smaller meals more frequently throughout the day (between 3 and 5 times), until they are at least six to twelve months of age.

As your puppy is growing, he or she requires more nutrients and calories than an adult dog, which is the reason why puppy foods contain higher levels of protein and fat to support optimal growth, as well as some added nutrients, such as DHA, which is an omega fatty acid found in mother's milk.

 If your dog is sharing the home with a cat, make sure that the dog cannot eat the cat's food because cat food is too high in protein for a dog and may cause the dog's hair to fall out.

Once your puppy reaches adulthood (between 10 and 12 months), he or she will not need as many calories. Unless they are highly active, continuing to feed rich puppy food to an adult dog may quickly lead to excessive weight gain, which means that the appropriate time to transition to adult food is important.

TIP *Labradoodles can be considered adults after about a year. While he or she may still be growing after this time, at the 12-month mark you can begin feeding your dog adult food.*

Feeding Adults

Choose foods that list high-quality meat protein as the main ingredient and, depending on your dog's particular energy level, feed between 2 and 3% of their body weight every day. While some dogs may prefer one meal a day,

most will appreciate morning food (after a walk) and evening food (after a walk).

Be careful not to get caught up in "convenience" when you're out grocery shopping for yourself, and decide to buy your dog's food at the same place, because most grocery stores tend to carry inferior brands of dog food.

Instead, make the time to visit your local pet store, talk with educated representatives, avoid grains and other unwanted fillers, and choose quality sources of meat protein for healthy puppies and dogs, including beef, buffalo, chicken, duck, fish, hare, lamb, ostrich, pork, rabbit, turkey, venison, or any other source of wild meaty protein.

Treats

There is an almost endless display of dog treat choices lining the shelves of every feed and pet store, and it can be an overwhelming task to choose wisely. When you want to do the best for your dog, the confusion surrounding choosing treats can be simplified if you keep one simple rule in mind. *Simply choose treats that contain only one ingredient or very few ingredients.*

Whatever reason you choose to give treats to your dog, be aware that treating our dogs too often throughout the day can cause them to become overweight, and/or we may create a picky eater who will no longer want to eat their regular meals. Doesn't it make sense that if you got to eat only your favourite tasty treats throughout the day, that you would be much less excited about consuming a meal that pales by comparison come dinner time?

DID YOU KNOW? *Researchers in Sweden have discovered that dogs were happier when they had to earn their treats as a reward for completing a task, rather than just being given a treat for looking cute. Just like us humans who get that happy "eureka" moment when we finally solve a problem, the same is true for our canine counterparts. The Labradoodle is the perfect dog for positive training methods that involve treat reinforcement.*

Dangerous Treats

Always carefully read labels so that you know exactly where the treats you may choose for your dog are being manufactured, because not all countries have the most stringent manufacturing protocols. Further, there are many treats that you absolutely should NOT be feeding to your dog, even though he or she may like them, including:

Rawhide (pictured) is soaked in an ash/lye solution to remove every particle of meat, fat and hair and then further soaked in bleach to remove any remaining traces of the ash/lye solution. Now that the product is no longer technically considered food, it no longer has to comply with food regulations.

The wet rawhide is shaped into chews, and once these chews dry, they shrink to approximately 25% of their original size before arsenic-based products are then used as preservatives, and antibiotics and insecticides are added to kill any lingering bacteria.

While rawhide chews are tough and long lasting, when a dog chews a rawhide treat, they end up ingesting many harsh chemicals. Also, when your dog swallows a piece of rawhide, that piece can swell up to four times its size inside your dog's stomach, which can cause anything from mild to severe gastric blockages that could become life threatening and require emergency surgery.

As much as it might be convenient for you to be able to give your dog or puppy a treat that will occupy them for a considerable time, if it's rawhide, just say "NO".

Pig's Ears (pictured) are very attractive to most dogs that will eagerly devour them, and they're "natural" because they're ears, so what could be wrong? Actually, these are thin, crispy and very high in fat, which can cause stomach upsets, vomiting and diarrhoea. Further, sharp pieces can break off and cause perforations in the mouth or become stuck in a dog's throat or digestive tract.

Also, pig ears are usually highly processed and preserved with unhealthy chemicals (to kill bacteria), that concerned dog guardians will NOT want to feed their dogs. Just say "NO".

Hoof Treats (pictured) are actual bison, cow, horse and pig hooves that humans believe are healthy, *"natural"* treat choices for their dogs. In truth, after processing with harsh chemicals, preservatives and antibiotics, they retain little, if any, of their *"natural"* qualities.

Also, hooves are very hard and can cause chipping or breaking of your dog's teeth as well as perforations in the mouth, throat or intestines, or blockages in your dog's intestines. Again, just say "NO".

Healthy Treats

Since there are so many healthy treat choices available, there's really no excuse for feeding your dog dangerous toxic, nutrient-deficient, unhealthy treats that could harm them. When you become a label reader, this will help to make sure the treats you may be choosing for your dog are of the highest quality. Examples of healthy treats include:

Hard Treats: come in many varieties of shapes, sizes and flavors for different sized dogs, and will help to keep your dog's teeth cleaner.

Soft Treats: are also available in endless sizes, varieties and flavors, suitable for all the different needs of our furry friends and are often smaller in size so they can be used for training purposes.

Dental Treats or Chews (pictured): are designed with the particular purpose of helping dogs to maintain healthy teeth and gums by exercising the jaw and massaging gums, while removing plaque build-up near the gum line that left unchecked can cause dental disease.

Dental disease can be entirely prevented if you are vigilant about good oral hygiene for your dog by brushing his or her teeth every day or two. Dog dental chews can be an excellent top-up between brushing or for dogs who will not let you get anywhere near their teeth without a great struggle.

There are both edible and non-edible varieties of dental chews and most dogs love the taste and think of them as a tasty treat. Non-edible chews are a bit like toys for many dogs and help to clean their teeth and exercise their jaws while satisfying their natural urge to chew at the same time.

Freeze-Dried and Jerky Treats (pictured): offer a tasty morsel most dogs find irresistible as they are usually made of simple, meaty ingredients, such as liver, poultry and seafood. Be careful about checking for added ingredients when choosing jerky treats, because they are often processed with too much salt.

Human Food Treats: many of our human foods contain unhealthy additives, such as salt, sugar and other ingredients that could be toxic and harmful to our fur friends. If you are going to feed your dog human food treats, make sure there are no additives than can be harmful to them.

As well, take some time to educate yourself about the many common human foods that are actually poisonous to our canine friends, such as grapes, raisins, onions and chocolate, to name a few.

Generally, the treats you feed your dog should not make up more than approximately 10% of their daily food intake, so make sure the treats you choose are high quality, with single or few ingredients because this can help to keep your dog both happy and healthy.

The Right Food for Your Happy Labradoodle

"Dog Food" has markedly changed since1785, when the English Sportman's Dictionary described the best diet for a dog's health in an article entitled *"Dog"*. It was the writer's opinion at this time that the best food for a dog was a product called *"Greaves"*, described as "*the sediment of melted tallow made into cakes for dogs' food*".

From these insufficient beginnings, commercially manufactured dog food has become a massively lucrative industry that has only fairly recently evolved beyond feeding our dogs the cheap and convenient dregs of human leftovers.

Even today, the majority of dog food choices often have far more to do with being convenient for humans to store and serve, than it does with being a diet truly designed to be a nutritionally balanced, healthy food choice for our canine companions.

Educating yourself by talking to experts and reading everything you can find on the subject, plus taking into consideration several relevant factors, will help to answer the question of what is the best food for your dog.

For instance, where you live may dictate what sorts of foods are available, while other factors to consider will include the particular requirements of your dog, such as their age, energy and activity levels.

Our dogs are also suffering from many of the same life-threatening diseases that are commonly found in our human society (heart disease, cancer, diabetes, arthritis, obesity). These diseases are often directly related to over-feeding and/or eating genetically altered foods that are no longer pure, in favour of a convenient, processed and packaged diet that is quick and easy for us to serve.

The Raw Diet: raw feeding advocates believe that the ideal diet for their dog is one which would be very similar to what a dog living in the wild would have access to while foraging or hunting prey.

These canine guardians are often firmly opposed to feeding their dog any sort of commercially manufactured pet foods, because they consider these foods to be inferior substitutes, and for the most part, I would agree.

For instance, many guardians of high energy, working breed dogs will agree that their dogs thrive on a raw or BARF (Biologically Appropriate Raw Food) diet and strongly believe that the potential benefits of feeding a raw dog food diet are many, whether your dog is simply your loyal companion, or earning a daily working wage herding sheep all day, including:

- 🐾 Healthy, shiny coats
- 🐾 Decreased shedding
- 🐾 Fewer allergy problems
- 🐾 Healthier skin
- 🐾 Cleaner teeth

- 🐾 Fresher breath

- 🐾 Increased energy levels

- 🐾 Improved digestion

- 🐾 Smaller stools

- 🐾 Strengthened immune system

- 🐾 Increased mobility in arthritic pets

- 🐾 Increase or improvement in overall health

- 🐾 Longer life

A raw diet is a direct evolution of what dogs ate before they became our domesticated pets and before we turned toward commercially prepared, easy-to-serve dry dog food that required no special storage or preparation.

The Dehydrated Diet (pictured): is available in both raw and cooked meat forms, and these are usually air dried to reduce moisture and inhibit bacterial growth. The appearance of dehydrated dog food is very similar to dry kibble, which means that it can be both healthy for our dogs and convenient for us to serve.

Dehydrated recipes are made from fresh, whole foods that have been minimally processed. The result is a healthy and nutritionally balanced meal that retains more of the overall nutritional value, and will meet or exceed the daily dietary requirements of a healthy canine.

A dehydrated diet is a convenient way to feed your dog a nutritious diet, because all you have to do is add warm water and wait five minutes while the food re-hydrates so your dog can enjoy a warm meal.

The Kibble Diet (pictured): there is no mistaking that the convenience and relative economy of dry dog food kibble, which had its beginnings in the 1940's, continues to be the most popular food choice for many dog-friendly humans. Thankfully, there are now many high-quality kibble foods available.

The Right Bowl for the Labradoodle: there are many different types and categories of dog bowls, including Automatic Watering, Elevated, Ceramic, Stoneware, No Skid, No Tip, Slow Feeder, Stainless, Wooden and Travel Bowls.

Always purchase bowls that are the correct size for your particular dog, and consider an elevated dining table **(pictured)** so that their head is up from the floor because this can be more comfortable when eating and drinking.

Also, if your dog wolfs their food, or has a deep chest (like the Labradoodle probably will), it would be a good idea to consider a slow feeder type of bowl **(pictured)** to help slow down the speed at which they consume their food, so that they are not at risk for life-threatening bloat.

In a Nutshell

While making wise food and treat choices for your favourite furry friend can be overwhelming, understanding basic canine physiology and taking the time to consider all the many different types of food and treats available can go a long way toward helping to add many healthy and happy years to your dog's life.

As you are the sole provider and protector for your canine companion, it cannot be stressed strongly enough the importance of a well thought out choice when deciding what brand and type of food and treats you will feed your loyal fur friend.

Carefully choosing food and treats and being careful to not overfeed may not only increase the length of your dog's life by helping to prevent unwanted health conditions (such as allergies, obesity, high blood pressure or bladder stones), well thought out food choices will provide your dog with optimal health so they can feel good and live a happy life!

Chapter 8: Care of the Happy Labradoodle

"When you adopt a dog, you have a lot of very good days, and one very bad day."
— W. Bruce Cameron

There are some situations that you might not at first associate with the safety of your happy Labradoodle. For instance, imagine you're travelling by vehicle on a daily basis without being protected by a seatbelt or an airbag. Would you feel safe? Roaming about inside a moving vehicle is the reality for far too many of our furry friends, because we humans often forget to think about vehicle safety for our dogs.

Further, how about going for months without brushing your teeth, cutting your nails, or washing your hair. This is another sad reality for many dogs, because their humans are not aware of how important it is to keep their canine fur friends well groomed. How happy and comfortable do you think such an ill cared for dog would be?

The following few paragraphs outline safe travelling, licensing, insurance and grooming requirements, all of which can help to ensure that your Labradoodle is safe, legal, better cared for at the vet's office and is well groomed.

As far as vehicle travel is concerned, if your dog is safely secured when travelling, they might not be dead or seriously injured should you be involved in a vehicle accident. We humans wear seatbelts to be safe and we need to think about safe vehicle travel for our best fur friends, too.

Being legal means buying a yearly license for your dog, and if your dog is properly licensed, that license tag they are wearing means that they will be returned to you should they go missing. This is a much happier dog than one spending who knows how long behind bars at a rescue or SPCA facility.

Further, if you have purchased a pet health insurance plan, chances are that your dog will be better cared for at the vet's office, because you won't have to worry about whether or not you can afford to take them, and this will most likely mean a healthier companion.

Last but not least, when your dog is regularly groomed, their coat and skin will look and feel better, and they won't suffer from tooth problems or sore joints from nails that are too long.

Tips for Keeping Your Dog Safe

Not So Safe Harness Restraints: is your canine companion really safe when buckled into a safety harness for travel inside vehicles? You might not be aware that many of the dog harnesses in the marketplace have a 100% failure rate.

If you are having difficulties finding a safety harness that has actually been strength and crash tested (i.e. optimal choice), the safest travel arrangement for any dog is to secure them inside a kennel that is bolted to the floor or secured with the vehicle's seatbelt system.

Remember that a dog travelling in the front passenger seat, even one secured with a crash tested safety harness, may still sustain injuries (and even death) during an accident if the 100 mph force of the airbag strikes them.

Kennels: a dog kennel or crate will easily fit on the back seat of most vehicles and can be secured with the vehicle's restraint system. A Labradoodle (or any dog) riding inside a kennel that is secure inside your vehicle will have the best protection in the case of a rollover accident, plus you will avoid the fines some locations are now levying when guardians permit their dogs to freely roam about or sit on a lap inside a moving vehicle because it's considered a distraction that can cause an accident. When you get a puppy used to this type of vehicle travel at an early age, they will happily accept it and be a much safer traveller for their entire life.

Air Travel: while the Labradoodle puppy may be small enough to fit into a soft Sherpa bag for travel inside an airplane cabin (as carry-on baggage), as an adult he or she will usually be too large. Any puppies or dogs that are too large to fit comfortably inside a Sherpa travel bag will need to be transported inside a heated cargo hold.

Licensing: when you purchase your dog a yearly license, and you attach this identifying tag to their collar, they will be considered legal. Any dog that should become lost when wearing a license tag will have a much higher possibility of being returned to you, instead of spending their last few days behind bars at the local SPCA or rescue facility.

Pet Health Insurance: purchasing health insurance for your dog means that they will usually live a longer, healthier and happier life, because they will receive better and often more frequent care throughout their lifetime.

Be aware that it's a good idea to begin insurance when your dog is a young puppy, because waiting until they are older will mean that your monthly premiums will be considerably higher.

Puppy Proofing

As your dog's guardian, it will be your responsibility to make sure that your Labradoodle's needs are taken care of, and this all begins with prepping your home for their arrival by puppy-proofing to keep him or her safe.

Next, you will need to learn what food and how often to feed your puppy and when to transition them to an adult dog food formula (previous chapter). You will also need to take regular care of your dog's grooming requirements, which is discussed later on in this chapter.

When it comes time to prepare your home for a new puppy or dog, start by walking through your home and viewing it through the much lower vantage point of a puppy's or dog's eyes to identify potential dangers. Here's a list of some of the things you may need to do:

- 🐾 Store cleaning products where your puppy cannot reach them or put them in a locked cabinet.

- 🐾 Put all trash in a can with a tight-fitting lid or keep it secured in a cupboard.

- 🐾 Store open food containers in your pantry or cupboards – anything left out needs a lid.

- 🐾 Tie up or bundle any enticing electrical and blind cords so your puppy cannot chew on them.

- 🐾 Pick up small objects from the floor – they are a choking hazard for a curious puppy.

- 🐾 Cover open bodies of water (such as the toilet, bathtub, outdoor ponds, swimming pools, etc.).

- 🐾 Put all medications and other toiletries where your puppy cannot reach them, such as in the medicine cabinet and use childproof bottles.

- 🐾 Make sure none of your house plants or plants in your yard are toxic to dogs – if there are any suspect plants or flowers, remove them, move them out of reach, or fence them off.

- 🐾 Keep your windows and doors securely closed when your puppy is roaming around – close doors, use baby gates or pet gates to keep them away from off-limits areas where you do not want them to wander or where they might fall down a set of stairs.

- ❧ If you have a cat, keep the litter box where your puppy cannot reach it, so he or she does not eat the clumps.

- ❧ Dispose of all food waste properly so your puppy cannot get it – this is especially important for chicken bones and foods that are harmful to dogs.

- ❧ Store all lawn and garden tools where your puppy cannot get to them and make sure they will not fall over if your puppy bumps into them.

- ❧ If you have a yard, consider adding a fence to keep your puppy in.

- ❧ Never leave them alone in a back yard, because even a fenced yard is little deterrent to a strong and motivated Labradoodle who has no fear of heights and is smart enough to figure out how to climb fences or open latches and escape.

- ❧ Avoid using toxic chemical fertilizers, pesticides, or herbicides anywhere your puppy could be exposed – this includes toxic carpet and floor cleaning products.

Once you have puppy-proofed your home, the next step is to set up your puppy's area. You can choose a small room or use a puppy playpen to cordon off a section of a larger room.

Place your puppy's crate and dog bed in the playpen area as well as their food, water bowls and toys. You will want to put your pup in this area when you cannot actively watch him or her so they are less likely to get into trouble.

While your puppy is very young, when you cannot closely watch them, such as when you need to take a shower, you may also want to confine him or her to their crate until they are housetrained.

Grooming Your Dog

Regular grooming is important for every happy and healthy dog, because it keeps them clean, and their skin moisturized and bug free, plus grooming time can alert you to any problems before they become more serious.

Traditionally, the Labradoodle will have an ever-growing coat, which will require weekly brushing to remove debris and tangles between full grooming sessions.

Hair Brushing Technique

- ❖ Use a soft bristle brush to brush out your dog's coat at least twice a week.

- ❖ Start at the base of the neck and work your way down the back and sides, always brushing in the direction of hair growth.

- ❖ Next, brush down each leg then have your dog roll over so you can brush out their underside. Don't forget the tail and also their face area.

Whether you decide to learn how to fully groom and clip your dog yourself, or will prefer to take him or her to the local doggy spa, in between full grooming sessions you will need minimal equipment to keep the coat of your happy dog looking his or her best.

If you're just keeping on top of weekly brushing, all you will need is a soft bristle brush, and perhaps a flea comb (just in case). If you're planning to do all your dog's grooming yourself, see *"Grooming Equipment You Will Need"* on the next page.

Also, it will be very important to get the Labradoodle (or any dog), used to their grooming routine early on, because during their lifetime there are many grooming procedures you will need to keep on top of. Otherwise, every time your dog needs to be bathed, brushed, clipped or have their nails shortened or their teeth brushed will end up being a traumatic experience for both dog and human that can last for many years. Start them off right so you can both enjoy grooming time.

I've been asked to groom dogs that have been kicked out of every grooming salon simply because their owners did not take the time to introduce the puppy to bath time, nail trimming and hair clipping procedures at a young age.

I can tell you from much personal experience that having to groom a writhing, screaming dog that is all teeth, because they are fighting the procedure, is hell on wheels, and the very worst case I ever encountered was with a dog weighing only 4 pounds (1.8 kg). Try going through this with an unwilling, much more muscular, heavier and athletic Labradoodle, and you will very soon be wishing your companion were a chia pet.

<u>Grooming Equipment You Will Need</u>

A standard arsenal of equipment for the DIY groomer that will help you keep your dog looking their best between clipping sessions will include the following:

Soft Bristle brush (pictured) – is the ideal tool for removing dirt and debris from the Labradoodle's coat, while at the same time distributing natural oils to keep the coat looking healthy and shiny.

Nail clippers (pictured) or a slow-speed Dremel™ type rotary pet nail grinder will be tools you need to use every couple of weeks or more, depending on how quickly your dog's nails grow, their activity level and what types of surfaces they may be regularly walking on. The nail grinder is perfect for smoothing the sharp edges that nail clippers leave, and if you are vigilant with regular use of this type of grinding tool, you may never have to clip.

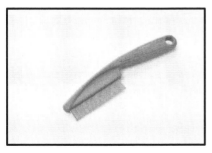

Flea comb (pictured) – while you may never need one, as the name suggests, these combs are designed for the specific purpose of removing tiny mites or fleas from a dog's coat. Usually small in size for manoeuvring in tight spaces, they are made of plastic or metal and the teeth are placed closely together to trap and remove hiding pests.

Tick Twister (pictured) – hopefully your dog won't ever get a tick, but if they do, this is a simple device for painlessly, easily and quickly removing blood sucking ticks that have imbedded themselves in your dog's skin.

Grooming Products You Will Need

When bathing and grooming your dog yourself, you will need to purchase shampoos, conditioners, creams, lotions, wipes, sprays and powders that are specially formulated for dogs.

Shampoos: NEVER make the mistake of using human shampoo or conditioner that has a pH balance of 5.5, for bathing your dog. Our canine companions have an almost neutral pH balance of 7.5, and any shampoo with a lower pH will be harmful to your dog, because it will strip the natural oils and be too harshly acidic for their skin and coat. If you use human products on your dog, this can cause itchy skin problems that will make your dog very unhappy.

Conditioners: take the extra few minutes to condition your dog's coat after shampooing, because this will not only make the coat look and feel better, it will also add many additional benefits, including:

- ❖ Preventing the escape of natural oils and moisture
- ❖ Keeping the coat cleaner for a longer period of time
- ❖ Repairing a dull, damaged or dry coat
- ❖ Restoring a soft, silky feel to the coat
- ❖ Helping the coat dry more quickly
- ❖ Protection from the heat of the dryer and breakage of hair

The benefits of spending the extra time to condition your dog's coat will be appreciated by both yourself and your dog that will have overall healthy, moisturized skin and a coat with a smooth feel and natural shine.

Bathing your dog:

- To bathe your dog, simply fill your bathtub with a few inches of lukewarm water and place your dog in it – you can put a bath mat or towel down to keep him or her from slipping. Smaller dogs can be easily bathed in a deep sink.

- Then, carefully check the temperature of the water on your wrist so that it is not too hot, and use a cup or a hand sprayer to wet down your dog's coat and work a little bit of dog-friendly shampoo into a thick lather. Don't forget the face, and ears.

- Rinse the coat well until the coat is completely free of all shampoo suds, and squeeze out the excess water with your hands.

- Apply canine conditioner and work it through the coat with your hands, and then rinse the coat thoroughly with warm water before squeezing out excess water and towelling your dog dry.

- If it's a cold day, it's a good idea to use a hairdryer on a warm setting to completely dry the coat. Puppies can especially get cold quickly after a bath.

- Unless your dog gets dirty, you should only plan to bathe him or her once every 4 to 6 weeks because bathing too often can dry out your dog's skin and coat.

<u>Oops, My Dog Has Fleas</u>

Perhaps you haven't been paying attention and now realize that your dog is suffering from an infestation of irritating, biting fleas. Now is the time to bathe your dog with shampoo containing pyrethrum (a botanical extract found in small, white daisies) or a shampoo containing citrus, cedar or tea tree oil.

Also, you can bathe and spray them with the non-toxic and highly effective CedarCide products, which can also be used to spray down their bedding and any carpets in the home. This highly effective product will kill fleas (or other crawly creatures) on contact without harming anyone.

CedarCide is a trusted company that makes 100% safe, organic products to control biting pests on your furry friends without the worry of toxic, harmful chemicals that are not good for you, your children or your canine companions because it's safe to use on dog and human alike. It's also a great mosquito deterrent for humans when camping.

Simply spray it on and bugs of any sort that come into contact with the solution will be instantly dead, while your dog's coat will be shiny and fresh smelling, like the inside of a cedar chest.

Nail Care

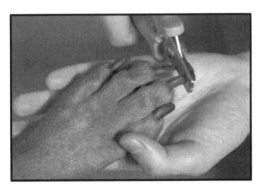

Many canine guardians are neglectful when it comes down to taking regular care of their dog's toenails. This is often because they're not comfortable with the process. With a little practise, you can get good at trimming your dog's nails and there are many online videos dedicated to showing humans how to do this properly. Leaving a dog's nails too long can lead to many problems later in life, such as painful joints, back pain and difficulty walking, which will make for a very unhealthy and unhappy dog.

Do yourself and your dog a favour, and purchase a professional quality pair of medium-sized, scissor-type nail clippers with a safety stop and learn how to properly use them. If you don't, your dog's nails will soon be too long and the vein inside the nail will also grow too long and you will be unable to keep them as short as they should be.

 Get your puppy used to having their nails trimmed at an early age. Purchase a pair of "nail scissors" which are much smaller and easier to handle for tinier nails, and simply snip off the sharp curved end of the nail.

Depending on the types of surfaces your dog is walking on, you should plan to clip your dog's nails approximately every two weeks. When trimming the nails, be sure to only snip the tip. You don't want to accidentally cut into the vein, because this will be painful for your dog and will cause the nail to bleed. If your dog does not usually walk on rough surfaces, you may have to clip or use a rotary sander more often.

Steps For Nail Clipping

- 🐾 Hold your dog's paw firmly but gently.

- 🐾 Trim the nail below the quick at a 45° angle, cutting small amounts at a time.

- 🐾 Trim small slices until you reach the white inside the nail with a small black dot at the centre. If you can't see the dot yet, and all you are seeing is completely white, you can cut a bit more.

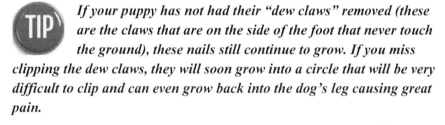

If your puppy has not had their "dew claws" removed (these are the claws that are on the side of the foot that never touch the ground), these nails still continue to grow. If you miss clipping the dew claws, they will soon grow into a circle that will be very difficult to clip and can even grow back into the dog's leg causing great pain.

Styptic Powder: You will always want to avoid causing any pain when trimming your dog's toenails, because you don't want to cause trauma and destroy their trust in you regularly performing this necessary task.

However, sometimes accidents do happen. Therefore, if you clip too short, and accidentally cut into the vein in the toenail, know that you will cause your dog pain, and that the toenail will bleed. Therefore, for those just in case times, keep some styptic powder (often called *"Kwik Stop")* in your grooming kit.

Dip a moistened finger into the yellow powder and apply it with a little pressure to the end of the bleeding nail. This is the quickest way to stop a nail from bleeding in just a few seconds.

Some dogs prefer having their nails trimmed with a rotary "Dremel" type of device that literally sands down the excess nail. There are several benefits inherent in using this type of tool for keeping your dog's nails trimmed, including: (a) it is easier to avoid cutting into the vein; (b) many dogs prefer it because there is no squeezing or clicking sound; (c) you can smoothly round the nails so there will be no sharp edges; and (d) when you use this tool every week, you can trim shorter and will never have to actually clip the nails.

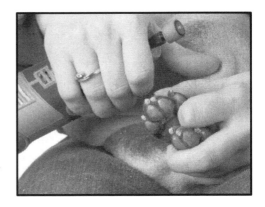

TIP *Keep in mind that if you decide to trim your dog's nails this way, you MUST purchase a "doggy Dremel-type" tool made especially for this purpose (pictured), because using your shop Dremel will harm your dog's nails as it is too high speed and will burn the nails.*

Ear Care

While dogs can often suffer from painful ear infections, paying attention and keeping your dog's ears clean and dry (especially after bathing or swimming) can go a long way toward preventing this type of unhappy health issue. If you notice your dog scratching at their ears, moaning, crying or constantly shaking their head, it's time for a trip to the vet's office. Make sure that you keep ear powders, wipes and cleaning solutions in your grooming kit, because with proper preventative care, you can help to prevent your dog from ever having to suffer from an irritating and painful ear infection.

Ear Powders: can be purchased at any pet store, and are designed to help keep your dog's ears dry while at the same time inhibiting the growth of bacteria that can lead to infections. Ear powders are also used when removing excess hair growth from inside a dog's ear canal, as the powder makes it easier to grip the hair.

Ear Cleaning Solutions: your local pet store will usually offer a wide variety of ear cleaning creams, drops, oils, rinses or wipes specially formulated for cleaning your dog's ears.

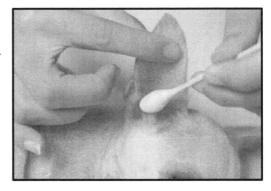

In addition, there are many

simple home remedies that will just as efficiently clean your dog's ears without the high price tag. These include Witch Hazel, a 50:50 solution of Organic Apple Cider Vinegar and Purified Water, or a 50:50 solution of Hydrogen Peroxide and Purified Water.

Cleaning your dog's ears

- Lift your dog's ear, holding it between your thumb and forefinger to get a good look inside the ear.

- Check for redness, discharge or bad smell. While it's normal to see a small amount of light-coloured wax, if there's a large amount, the ears are red, or there appears to be any sort of discharge or a bad smell, this is a sign of a problem that will require immediate veterinary attention.

- Gently wipe around the entrance of the ear canal with damp cotton wool, removing dirt or excess wax.

- Insert the tip of the ear cleaning solution bottle into the ear canal making sure not to insert it too far, and then squeeze to release the ear cleaner.

- Massage the base of the ear to help the cleaner pass inside the ear canal, and then wipe away any excess with damp cotton wool.

- Repeat the same process for the other ear.

- If there is an infection and your vet has prescribed drops, it's best to apply them straight after you've finished cleaning the ears. This will ensure that the medicine will enter the ear effectively and be absorbed without being blocked by excess wax.

Teeth Care

Another greatly overlooked area in your happy dog's health, that can cause many entirely preventable problems, is ensuring that their teeth are clean and properly looked after, so that they don't suffer from loose or broken teeth, and plaque build-up that leads to painful gum disease.

We humans know how miserable a toothache can be – imagine your poor dog that cannot tell you how unhappy they are.

Don't let yourself become one of those guardians that use the excuse that *"My dog doesn't like it"* when they try to brush their dog's teeth. Of course they don't *"like"* it, but they will not like lost teeth or painful gum disease even more.

Do NOT give up and overlook the fact that in order to keep the entire dog healthy, they <u>must</u> have healthy teeth and the only way to ensure this, is to commit to making the time to brush your dog's teeth every day or two.

Canine Toothpastes: are flavoured with beef or chicken that will hopefully appeal to the dog's taste buds, and some contain baking soda, which is the same mild abrasive found in many human pastes, and are designed to gently scrub the teeth.

Other types of canine toothpastes are formulated with enzymes that are designed to work chemically by breaking down tartar or plaque in the dog's mouth. While these pastes don't need to be washed off your dog's teeth and are safe for them to swallow, whether or not they remain on the dog's teeth long enough to do any good might be debatable. It's actually the brushing that is the most effective deterrent to painful gum disease or lost teeth.

Just as effective for killing germs, whitening and cleaning your dog's teeth, and much less expensive than fancy pastes, is old-fashioned hydrogen peroxide; you can also combine hydrogen peroxide (3% food grade), Aloe Vera juice (1:1) with a little bit of baking soda.

How can I brush my dog's teeth?

In the beginning, it's important to get your dog used to the toothpaste and to the whole brushing experience. Here is the technique I use:

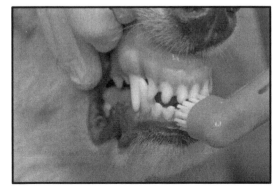

* Check your dog's teeth and gums often

to see what is normal so you can spot any issues or problems.

- During the first few days, hold your puppy or dog as you would normally when you are petting him or her.

- Gently stroke the outside of the cheeks with your finger for 1 or 2 minutes.

- After each session, reward your dog with praise and a treat they like. For the next few days, after your dog has become comfortable with this activity, place a small amount of toothpaste on your finger, let your dog try the flavour and rub it on their teeth and gums.

- Next, you should introduce your dog to a canine toothbrush or finger brush.

- Apply a pea-sized amount of toothpaste that has been specially formulated for dogs on the brush. Gently lift your dog's upper lip and place the brush against an upper tooth.

- With a slow circular motion, brush gently only that tooth and the adjoining gum line.

- Every following day gradually increase the number of teeth being brushed. Remember to go slowly, and do not continue beyond your dog's point of comfort.

- Build up to 30 seconds of brushing per side.

- The easiest way to do this is to go straight, pushing the brush gently from front to back along the gum line. Next, add in the gentle circular motion.

- You do not have to brush the inside of the teeth, as the tongue keeps that side relatively free of plaque.

- After each session reward your dog with a treat and lots of praise.

- Ideally, brushing should be carried out every day, but if you miss 1-2 days per week, that would not be a big concern.

The easiest and most effective way to brush a dog's teeth is with an electric toothbrush (the rotary type) that does all the work for you. You can slowly introduce this method, just as you did

with the manual brush, and once your dog gets used to the buzzing, all you have to do is hold the brush against their teeth.

Paw Care

If your dog runs over sharp barnacles on the beach, jogs with you on hard road surfaces, or over other rough terrain, this can cause cuts and scrapes and very rough surfaces on the paws. If you live in a hot climate, be aware that sidewalks, road surfaces and

sandy beaches can get extremely hot for your dog's feet.

Paw Creams: depending upon activity levels and the types of surfaces our canine counterparts usually walk on, they may suffer from cracked or rough pads. You can restore resiliency and keep your dog's paws in healthy condition by regularly applying a cream or lotion especially formulated for dogs that will help to protect their paw pads. The perfect time to do this is just after you've clipped or sanded down their nails.

Doggy Wipes

Getting your dog used to a quick freshen-up between bath times with moist doggy wipes is a good way to get him or her used to regular grooming sessions. Also, doggy wipes are perfect for a quick clean-up of eyes and face in the morning, and easily removing the dust and debris of the day before bed.

In a Nutshell

Learning a simple routine that will keep your Labradoodle safe, and being aware of what's involved in proper grooming sessions will go a long way toward helping your dog to live a long, happy and healthy life.

While for many people the concept of grooming a dog conjures up notions of brushes and bows, it is in fact an important and vital element for the overall health and wellbeing of every dog.

Whether you decide to bathe, clip the coat and trim the nails yourself, or hire someone to do it for you on a regular basis, these activities along with brushing your dog's teeth and taking the time to brush the coat between full grooming sessions are essential tasks that YOU will be required to do for your dog every day or two.

Also, you might want to keep in mind that carrying out these essential grooming procedures yourself will strengthen the bond between you and your best fur friend while alerting you to any possible diseases or conditions early on that could help your dog feel better.

Chapter 9: Are YOU the Ideal Labradoodle Guardian?

*"A dog is the only thing on earth that
loves you more than he loves himself."*
— Josh Billings

If you have not chosen wisely when sharing your life with a canine companion, it's not only your dog that will be frustrated and unhappy, because the ripple effect can be far reaching. While your dog will not be happy and neither will you, you will also be setting yourself, your family, your friends, strangers you may encounter when out walking, and your neighbours up for many years of stress, guilt and unhappiness.

You may not have considered that bringing a dog into your family is a substantial lifestyle change that can have far reaching consequences. Since it IS such a large lifestyle change, it's vitally important that you take an accurate and honest look at your own energy level and lifestyle, ask yourself some serious questions and not cut corners when taking the time to carry out plenty of research about the breed of dog you may be considering.

Sharing your life with a canine friend should never be a lightly undertaken endeavour that is a whim or spur of the moment decision, because your children are begging for a dog, or because you like the colour of a dog's coat, their pleading eyes, or the sweet expression on their face.

Do You Have What It Takes?

Before you can learn how to become your dog's best friend and ideal guardian, you need to first be honest about your lifestyle, and have no doubt in your mind that you have the energy, commitment, time and skill level necessary so that you can raise a happy dog. Once this is established in the affirmative, you then need to know how to choose the right breed of puppy or dog for your particular lifestyle.

Choosing the <u>right</u> puppy for your family is more important than you might have first imagined, and far too many people forget to consider how vital it is to choose a puppy or dog based on an honest assessment of compatibility with their own energy and lifestyle.

For instance, many humans choose a puppy (or older dog) for all the <u>wrong</u> reasons, including because:

- ❧ they like what it looks like

- ❧ the breed may currently be popular

- ❧ they like that this dog's coat is easy care

- ❧ they like the beautiful pattern of a dog's coat

- ❧ the breed appeared on TV or in a movie they enjoyed

- ❧ their parents had the same kind of dog when they were a child

- ❧ a friend or someone they admire has the same breed

- ❧ they feel sorry for a homeless dog

- ❧ a friend or family member can no longer keep their dog

- ❧ the children are begging for a dog

- ❧ someone was selling puppies on a street corner

While some of the above-noted reasons can be honourable, the most important reasons for choosing to share your life with a particular canine companion has not been overlooked.

In order to make an informed, intelligent choice that will make everyone happy, all you need to do is take an honest look at your life as it is today and then how you envision it might be during the next ten to fifteen years, followed by asking yourself several very important questions, including:

Activity – Do I lead a highly active, medium or low-intensity life? Do I work at home, or does my job keep me away from home for many hours every day? Does my leisure time activity find me out jogging the streets every morning or hiking local mountain trails, or does it keep me in front of the computer or on the couch watching movies?

"Can't take my dog?! But I don't even know HOW to run without my dog!"

Travel – Do I travel a lot for work or pleasure? If you do, perhaps you should choose a small dog that can travel with you in the plane cabin. If you can't take your loyal dog with you on your travels, they will be unhappy without you or you will have greatly increased expenses, because you will have to hire a dog sitter to care for them or leave them in a kennel.

Special Needs – do I have the extra finances required to keep a Labradoodle well-groomed and cared for? Am I able to keep this boisterous, loyal dog at my side throughout most of every day? Do I have the time and fitness level to keep up with such an energetic dog?

Allergies – Do I have allergies? While this dog sheds their hair minimally, family members with allergies may still be allergic.

Time – Does my family take up all my spare time and are my children old enough to handle a puppy? A dog is like a child that never grows up and in order for them to be happy and well-behaved family members, they require a LOT of your daily time and attention.

Fitness – Am I physically fit and healthy enough to be out there walking and exercising a dog two to three times a day, every day, rain or shine, and much more during the puppy stage? Do I have the time to involve this highly energetic dog in a canine sport that will give them the mental stimulation this very smart dog needs?

Energy – Do I have a strong enough personality to keep this dog in check? Remember that this dog's parents both come from a retrieving background and they will need at least 1-2 hours of vigorous activity every day.

Cost – Am I able to afford the extra food costs, trips to the grooming parlour, health insurance, licensing, appropriate clothing and the veterinarian expenses that are part of being a conscientious guardian?

Commitment – Is the decision to bring a puppy or dog into my life a family decision, or just because the children, who may quickly lose interest, have been begging for a dog?

Why? – What is the number one reason why I want a dog in my life?

Once you ask yourself these important questions and honestly answer them, you will have a much more realistic understanding of whether or not you have what it takes to share your life with a dog, and perhaps also the beginning insight into the type of puppy or dog that would be best suited for you and your family.

If you're too busy for a dog, or choose the wrong dog that is not compatible with you or your family's energy and lifestyle this could be the beginning of problems. Consider that if you don't really have the time, finances, patience, right energy, expertise and commitment necessary to properly socialise, train, exercise, feed, groom, raise and care for a canine companion, you will inevitably end up with a family and a dog that are both frustrated and unhappy.

When a dog is bored, frustrated and unhappy, this will lead to behavioural issues, which will then lead to a stressed family, and angry neighbours. In a best-case scenario, there will be extra expenses to hire a professional to help you reverse unwanted behavioural problems.

Even worse, an incompatible choice can mean that you may end up in a lawsuit or contributing to the already overflowing crisis of yet another dog being abandoned at the local SPCA or kill shelter.

Once you have carried out all your homework, and absolutely determined that the highly energetic, strong, athletic and loving Labradoodle is the right dog for you (see next Section: The Ideal Guardian), rather than simply leaving it to chance, you need to choose the right puppy from the litter.

How to Choose Your Labradoodle Puppy

Generally speaking, when choosing a puppy out of a litter, look for one that is outgoing and friendly, rather than one who is overly bossy or timid and nervous.

Visit the breeder and take note of a puppy's social skills when they are amongst their littermates, because this will help you to choose the right puppy for your family. Puppies who demonstrate good social skills with their littermates are much more likely to become easy-going, happy adults who play well with other dogs.

When all the puppies can be observed together in a social setting, there are several important observations you can make, including:

Play – When the puppies are wrestling or play fighting, take notice of which puppies are comfortable both on top and on the bottom and which puppies seem to only like having the dominant on top position. Puppies who don't appear to mind the less aggressive posture of being on the bottom when wrestling with their littermates or who appear to be fine with either position, will usually play nicely with other dogs when they become adults.

Sharing – Observe which puppies try to be possessive and keep all the toys to themselves and which ones will share. Those who want to keep all other puppies away so that they can hoard the toys for his or herself may have tendencies to be more dominant or aggressive with other dogs, or even children, when food, treats or toys are involved as they become older.

Company – Notice which puppies seem to like the company of the other pups and which ones seem to be loners. Those who appear to enjoy the company of their littermates are less likely to become anti-social, and more likely to be interested in friendly socialising with other dogs as they mature.

Compassion – Observe the reaction of puppies that get yelped at when they bite or roughhouse too vigorously with another puppy. Puppies who stop or ease up when another puppy cries or yelps in pain are more likely to respond appropriately during rough adult play.

Sociability – Is the puppy you are interested in sociable with people? If he or she will not come to you, or seems to be nervous or afraid of strangers, this may develop into a fear/aggression problem that can escalate into biting or being aggressive toward strangers when they become more confident adults.

Handling – Is the puppy you are contemplating relaxed about being picked up or handled? A puppy that is not relaxed about being handled may become nervous or difficult around children or adults during daily interactions, when grooming is required, or when it's time to visit the veterinarian's office.

Is Your Happy Puppy Healthy?

While mental health is very important, you will also want to do all you can to determine if your chosen puppy is physically healthy.

Ask to see the breeder's veterinarian reports to satisfy yourself that the puppy has been examined and is as healthy as possible. Then, once you make your decision to share your life with a particular puppy, and they are old enough to go home with you, make an appointment with your own veterinarian for a complete examination and vaccination schedule.

Before you take your new puppy home, there are general signs of good physical health to be aware of, including the following:

Body Fat – a healthy puppy will look round and well fed, with an obvious layer of fat over their rib cage.

Breathing – a healthy puppy will breathe quietly, without coughing, sneezing, or wheezing.

Coat Condition – a healthy puppy will not be itchy and will have a soft coat with no dandruff, bald spots, dullness or greasiness.

Energy Level – a well-rested puppy will be alert, playful and energetic.

Hearing – a healthy puppy should react if you clap your hands, click your tongue or snap your fingers behind their head.

Genitals – a healthy puppy will not have any type of discharge visible in or around their anal or genital regions.

Mobility – a healthy puppy will walk and run normally without limping, wobbling, or appearing to be stiff, sore, unstable or weak.

Vision – a healthy puppy will have clear, bright eyes without crust or discharge and they should notice if a toy is tossed nearby or a ball is rolled within their field of vision.

The Ideal Guardian Profile

Once you've established that you have what it takes to share your life with a particular dog (by considering the questions in the previous Section), you might find the following information useful to help you determine whether the Labradoodle would truly be the right breed for you and your family.

This dog will be an excellent choice for moderate to high-energy individuals or families who live in a home with a yard or on a property or hobby farm, and may have children that understand how to respect a dog that has considerable daily mental and physical exercise needs.

This dog could be a loyal companion for active senior adults who have the knowhow and strong enough energy to raise a highly intelligent breed and have the energy, time and mobility required to provide this energetic and athletic companion with the vigorous daily physical exercise and mental stimulation they need.

Keep in mind that a well-socialised dog that heeds their guardian's word will usually be accepting toward both unknown dogs and humans; when not trained to follow their guardian's lead and not adequately socialised, any dog, even one like the Labradoodle that is usually friendly to all, could become dominant, or aggressive in unfamiliar situations. If you baby them too much and do not properly train or have strong enough energy yourself that this dog will eagerly follow, you could be responsible for them developing behaviour problems.

The ideal guardian for the Happy Labradoodle will be a person who is a naturally firm leader, and understands the importance of consistent rules and boundaries to keep this boisterous dog in check. This person may be retired or working at home, and will enjoy several energetic daily walks plus off leash time to let their dog freely run, and ideally some time for a vigorous canine sport.

Further, this guardian will also be aware of this dog's high stamina and strong desire to be occupied with interesting tasks, and that they may develop depression, frustration, a nervous disposition or separation anxiety (that leads to destructive behaviour, barking and escape attempts), if they are expected to spend long hours alone every day.

This ideal guardian will also understand the importance of early and on-going socialising, supervision and firm, fair training. This individual may be interested in teaching their companion tricks and/or a fun canine sport, and be willing to involve him or her in their own daily walking, biking, swimming, jogging or hiking routine.

As an example, this dog's guardian may be someone who takes his or her dog out for a brisk 30-minute walk, so they can empty their bladder and bowels first thing every morning before breakfast, rain or shine, plus engage in some supervised off-leash time where they can run freely chasing and retrieving a ball or socialising and safely playing with other dogs.

After returning home, everyone will have their breakfast and then (since you work at home or are retired) your dog can relax for a couple of hours while you work about the home. Before long it's noon and time to leash up your companion and head off for a longer walk or perhaps a hike. Depending on the weather, you may finish up at the lake or ocean side for a game of fetch in the water. If it's a hot day out, always carry water for your dog, and don't let them play too long.

Back home for a noon time dental snack for your dog and lunch for you, while you take time (depending on this dog's age) to teach basic commands, play a short game in the back yard, maybe teach some tricks, or head off to the local Agility or Flyball course.

Now it's about 4:00 pm and again it's time to get you and your dog outside for a 30-minute walk around the block, or perhaps hitch them up to a Springer bicycle jogger and let them jog beside your bicycle. Or if he or she is a large and very strong dog, perhaps some time to let them be the power for your dog powered scooter. Then, if it's not too hot or too cold out, perhaps another short stop at the park for socialising and running free with other dogs.

 Keep in mind that if you live where the winters are harsh and you have access to a treadmill, this super smart dog can quickly be taught to exercise indoors alongside you on a treadmill.

Back home and time to prepare evening meals for both dog and human, then after dinner (again depending on the age of your dog) perhaps a few more minutes of basic command and/or trick training before you head off to the local dog park for a game of Frisbee.

Now it's getting to be later evening and before bed you need to put your dog on leash and take them outside for a few minutes so they can drain out their bladder before bed.

Everyone now in his or her respective beds as both human and dog enjoy a relaxing and rejuvenating sleep before the start of the next day when you do this (or something similar) all over again.

Of course, this is just one scenario that would be excellent for the energetic and versatile Happy Labradoodle, and with a little imagination on your part, there are many others that would just as easily fit the bill quite nicely.

Also, don't forget to check out your local weekend canine sporting facilities, because once your dog is well socialised and trained to follow your lead, your weekend would be well spent teaching this robust dog how to run an Agility course, or perhaps participate in Advanced Obedience or even learn how to bring home the blue ribbons in a Dock Diving competition.

In a Nutshell

While choosing the right puppy is important, even more important is your ability to ask and honestly answer the questions outlined in this Chapter. Taking the time to be honest with yourself will help you to understand if you truly are a good fit for being the ideal guardian for this affectionate and energetic dog, who will be your devoted and loving companion for many years.

Always keep in mind that if you don't really have the time, right energy, commitment and knowledge necessary to properly socialise, train and raise this intelligent, bouncy and energetic companion (that includes mental and physical exercise), you will inevitably end up with an unhappy dog.

When a dog is mismatched with their human guardian, this can lead to a stressed dog, which can bring about health and behavioural issues. Along with these issues comes a stressed family, and often possibly angry neighbours or strangers you may meet when out walking your dog. If you are unable to figure out how to reverse unwanted behaviours, the next step may be extra expenses to hire a professional to help you work through these problems, which is, of course, only possible if YOU are able and willing to make the necessary changes in your life.

Chapter 10: Humans Can Make Mistakes

*"Heaven goes by favor. If it went by merit,
you would stay out and your dog would go in."*
— Mark Twain

Far too often we humans don't even realize we are the cause of creating unwanted behavioural problems in our canine companions. When we're not paying attention, or are simply not aware, we may actually be causing issues that could have been entirely avoided.

When not carefully raised, taught firm rules and boundaries and engaged in vigorous activities that build both body and mind, there are many possible situations or unwanted outcomes that may arise that might have been avoided.

Being aware of common "mistakes" that we humans can inadvertently make can go a long way toward preventing troubles later in life. For instance, we can fall short in areas such as:

- 🐾 not taking the time to properly socialise

- 🐾 not desensitizing our dog to loud noises

- falling prey to those staring eyes that they know how to work to their own advantage

- feeding too much

- leaving our loyal companion alone too much

- not exercising enough

- not finding ways to mentally challenge

- accidentally rewarding our dog at the wrong time

- allowing our dog to be the boss

- not being a strong enough leader for the breed we choose

- not having the knowledge we need to properly raise a dog

- not being aware of a particular breed's special needs

- not taking the time to teach basic rules and boundaries

- not being honest about our own energy level

- not being honest about how much time we can devote to a dog

All of these and more can create frustration and unwanted behaviours that could have been entirely avoided.

As well, not being aware of the adolescent craziness time in a young dog's life and how to get through it relatively unscathed, and many other less obvious mistakes, such as choosing the wrong collar or leash, allowing your dog to sleep in your bed, or free feeding can all result in the creation of unforeseen problems.

While we humans may be well intentioned, besides the obvious disasters that we can create when we don't properly train or socialise our canine friends, it's sometimes easy to make a lot of mistakes when raising our dogs that may cause our fur friends to needlessly suffer.

Let's begin with the more obvious *"Preventing Socialisation Behavioural Issues"* that can lead to unsettling problems later in life, and proceed further into areas of *"Accidental Rewards"* that may not be so obvious, then touch upon *"Basic Rules and Boundaries"* and *"Adolescent Craziness",* and finish this chapter with *"Less Obvious Human Mistakes".*

Preventing Socialisation Behavioural Issues

In order to prevent behavioural issues, we humans first need to understand how easy it is to inadvertently create them ourselves.

Consider that much of how your chosen dog learns to behave will depend entirely upon you, including how extensively they were socialised as a puppy and how much they are continually being socialised throughout their life.

Without proper socialisation, even the most naturally polite dog can become neurotic, overly bossy, nervous, unsociable, and learn to act out aggressively toward unknown dogs, smaller animals or people. This is a situation that can get any dog labelled nasty or even dangerous should they act out aggressively for any reason.

Many people don't realize how important it is to properly and continually socialise their dogs in several different areas.

 Without proper socialisation, many unwanted behavioural problems could become a daily occurrence.

Never make the mistake of thinking that you only need to socialise your puppy during the first few months of their life and that they will then be fine for the next 12 to 15 years, because all dogs, including the usually friendly Labradoodle, require constant socialising.

As well, once they reach adolescence, a dog's personality can really begin to assert itself, and this is when, without constant and vigilant daily socialising and training, and keeping on top of firm rules and boundaries, unwanted aggressive or anti-social tendencies may begin to rise to the surface.

Generally speaking, the majority of an adult dog's habits and behavioural traits will be formed between the ages of birth and one year of age. While it is even more important to introduce puppies to a wide variety of sights, sounds, smells and situations during the most formative period in their young life (usually the first 16 weeks), all dogs, no matter their age or breed, need to be exposed to different people, dogs, animals, places and unusual sights and sounds throughout their entire adult life.

Socialising With Unknown Dogs

Any dog, even one with a naturally friendly temperament, that is not regularly socialised may become timid, nervous, fearful, suspicious or overly bossy around unfamiliar or unusual dogs, animals, people or circumstances.

Daily on-leash dog walks are the perfect opportunities for your dog to see and possibly meet other dogs and different people, as well as practice proper behaviour when out and about.

Remember to take it slowly and never put your fur friend in an uncomfortable situation where he or she feels forced into being around other canines or situations they may find unsettling. Your dog should always be given the option to walk away, with plenty of space.

When socialising a young puppy, remember to introduce him or her first to the *more calm and friendlier* dogs. Introducing your small pup to an "in your face" type of dog that may be overly boisterous or not so friendly with other puppies or other dogs may result in a negative experience that could teach your dog to be fearful or to feel forced into taking an aggressive stance.

While the Labradoodle is usually eager to meet other dogs and people, depending upon their guardian's energy and degree of control, this dog may be overly boisterous, which may unsettle some dogs and cause them to react in an aggressive manner. I would suggest finding a local puppy class with around 8-10 other puppies, so that you can carefully supervise early socialising and guided play.

Socialising Between Puppies and Older Dogs

Many dogs don't get along particularly well with exuberant puppies who get all up in their face and bite at tails, lips and ears with those needle-sharp puppy teeth. While some older dogs may be more tolerant or simply move away and avoid, others may growl or even bite to discipline a rambunctious puppy.

Unfortunately, too many humans simply allow little puppies to run rampant and do whatever they like because they're small and so cute, when what they should be doing is gently disciplining their small bundle of fur. Puppies need to be taught what IS and what is NOT acceptable behaviour around other dogs.

When puppies are displaying wild, rambunctious energy and inflicting it upon another older dog that is not very appreciative of this crazy energy, this can place the puppy in a dangerous situation. When the human is not vigilant, the other dog may simply nip or give the puppy a bite that may scar them for life, which can go far beyond possible stitches.

When puppies are not taught to be respectful of older dogs and human guardians are not being careful to monitor socialising and play sessions, the puppy might get injured. If this happens, depending upon the temperament of the particular puppy and the degree of any sort of injury, there can be unwanted outcomes that could last a lifetime. For instance, a traumatic, scary experience between a puppy and an older dog can result in the puppy (a) becoming nervous and afraid of larger dogs or a particular type of dog, or (b) becoming aggressive toward other dogs as they grow up and gain their confidence.

Of course, we want to ensure that we socialise our puppies at an early age. However, we also need to be mindful of what's going on when a puppy meets another dog. It's important to carefully observe the body language of both, so that we can step in and stop the play or step it down a notch when it gets too much for either dog. Every puppy needs to learn to respect his or her elders and that can only happen if their guardian takes the lead and teaches their puppy to play nicely.

Socialising With Unknown People

Proper socialisation also means taking your puppy (or dog) everywhere with you and introducing them to many different people of all ages, sizes and ethnicities, so they will learn what is normal and acceptable behaviour in their daily life.

DO NOT get into the habit of always carrying a puppy or smaller dog. They need to walk on their own feet so that they don't develop unwanted behaviour problems, such as "armpit alligator" tendencies (snapping when someone stops to say hello) that can result from being in an elevated position where they feel they are in charge and must protect their human.

Also important, will be getting your puppy or dog used to the often loud and unpredictable actions of young children. You will want to closely supervise play, so that children are not accidentally being too rough or screaming in high-pitched voices, because this can be unsettling for a young puppy or dog that is unfamiliar with children.

Be especially careful when introducing your puppy to young children who may accidentally hurt your puppy, because you don't want your dog to become fearful of children as this could lead to aggression issues later on in life. While most Labradoodles are affectionate, gentle and tolerant with children, any dog can feel threatened by small children who do not understand how to respect a dog's personal space. Any dog that is pushed too far may feel the need to protect his or herself from a child that is hurting them or treating them too roughly.

Environmental Socialisation

It can be a BIG mistake not to take the time to introduce your Labradoodle puppy to a wide variety of different environments. When a dog is not comfortable with different sights, smells and sounds, this could cause them (and you) much stress and trauma later in their adult life.

Be creative and take your puppy to many different places when they are young, so that no matter where they travel, whether on leash along a crowded city sidewalk or freely running beside a deserted shoreline, they will be equally comfortable. Also, don't forget to train this dog to calmly accept travelling inside their kennel when driving anywhere so they can be safe and secure when on the road with you.

Some people only take their puppy into areas where they live and frequently travel. This can be a mistake because your dog also needs to be just as comfortable visiting areas you might not often visit, such as noisy construction sites, airports, a different park, or a petting zoo across town.

Your puppy needs to see all sorts of people, animals, sights, sounds and situations so that they will not become nervous or unsettled, should they need to travel with you outside of their familiar neighbourhood. Also, if you plan to regularly fly with your dog, if you wait until they are older before they have their first experience in the air, they could really freak out. Get them used to air travel, or any other mode of transportation that will be a common occurrence in your life, when they're still a young puppy.

Your dog will take their cues from you, which means that when you are calm and firmly in control of every situation, they will learn to trust and calmly follow your lead.

For instance, take them to a noisy construction site, to the airport where they can watch people and hear planes landing and taking off, to a local park where they can hear a crowd and see a baseball game, for a stroll beside a schoolyard at recess time when noisy children are out playing, or to the local zoo or farm and let them get a close up look at horses, pigs, chickens and ducks. Use your imagination.

Again, never think that socialisation only takes place when your dog is a young puppy, as proper socialisation is part of your dog's entire life.

Fear of Loud Noises

Many dogs can show extreme fear of loud noises, such as fireworks, sirens, thunderstorms or home security alarms, and may completely lose it. We humans need to learn how to either prevent this trauma in the first place or learn how to appropriately respond to a dog that is afraid of loud noises.

When you take the time to desensitize your dog to these types of noises when they are very young, it will be much easier on them during stormy weather, holidays such as Halloween or New Year's, when noisy fireworks are often a part of the festivities, when out on a walk and an ambulance, police or fire truck roars past with sirens loudly wailing, or when your fire or security alarm is activated.

REMEMBER: Loud, piercing noises will be very painful for a dog's sensitive ears, so use your hands to protect their ears if you're out walking when a vehicle with a blaring siren is roaring past.

Desensitization Devices: there are several ways you can help to desensitize your dog, so that they are not traumatized by high-pitched alarms, and loud, popping or banging noises or explosions, including the following:

CDs: you can purchase CD's that are a collection of loud sounds, such as vacuums or hoovers, airplanes, sirens, smoke alarms, fireworks, guns firing, people clapping hands, screaming children, and more (or you can easily make your own), that you can play while working in your kitchen or relaxing in your living room or lounge.

Begin by playing these sounds at a low level and then slowly increase the volume when you see that your dog is unaffected. When you play these sounds and pretend that everything is normal, the next time your puppy or dog hears these types of sounds elsewhere, they will not become upset or agitated because they will have already learned to ignore them.

Bubble Wrap: is also another simple way to desensitize a dog that is fearful of unexpected popping sounds. Show them the bubble wrap, pop a few of the cells and if they do not run away, give them a treat. Begin this exercise with the bubble wrap that has small, quieter cells, and then graduate them to the larger celled (louder) bubble wrap. You can also take things even farther by blowing up some small paper bags or balloons and loudly popping them in front of your dog, and if plan to hunt with them, you might take them to a local rifle range.

Thunder Shirts: some dogs will respond well to wearing a *"Thunder Shirt"*, which is specifically designed to alleviate anxiety or trauma associated with loud rumbling, popping or banging noises. The idea behind the design of the Thunder Shirt is that the gentle pressure it creates is similar to a hug that, for some dogs, can have a calming effect.

Relaxation Collars: there are basically two types of collars designed to help relax or calm an upset puppy or dog. One uses scent or calming pheromones, and the other uses species-specific music at appropriate decibel levels to calm a fearful or stressed dog.

TV or Radio: sometimes all that is required to calm a dog that is stressed by loud noises is to play your inside TV or Radio station with the sounds of relaxing music, louder than you might normally, to help disguise the exterior noise of fireworks or thunder.

FACT *Some dogs literally lose their minds and do things that make no logical sense when they're frightened by popping or screeching noises of fireworks and various alarms and start trembling, running or trying to hide and communicating with them becomes quite impossible.*

For instance, my dog, Boris, used to try and escape through the drain in the bathtub (go figure), because loud popping noises literally caused him to lose his mind.

Make certain that your dog cannot harm itself trying to escape from these types of scary noises, and if possible, calmly hold them until they begin to relax.

Make sure that YOU are acting appropriately yourself, by not panicking or having weak, *"feeling sorry"* or *"angry and frustrated"* energy around an upset dog, because this will only make matters worse.

Consider that when the person who is supposed to be a dog's support system is also feeling weak or acting unstable, the dog will have nowhere to turn. Instead, support a stressed or frightened dog by pretending that nothing is wrong and if you must talk to them, do so in a calm, yet assertive voice.

Never underestimate the importance of taking the time to continually (not just when they are puppies) socialise and desensitize your dog to all manner of sounds. Doing so will help curb a dog's tendency to sound off at every little noise, which will make everyone happier in the future, while teaching them to be a calm and well-balanced member of your family in every situation.

Accidental Rewards

Many times, we humans are guilty of accidentally rewarding our puppies and dogs for engaging in types of behaviour we are embarrassed about or not happy with. The following outlines some of the more obvious things we may be doing that can actually be rewarding, and thus encouraging more of an unwanted behaviour.

Aggression Rewards

Many people unknowingly get into the habit of accidentally rewarding their puppies or dogs for displaying nervousness, fear, barking, growling or lunging at another dog or person by picking them up, talking soothingly, or offering them a treat. I see this happen all too frequently.

For instance, many people simply pick up their dog when they are acting out toward another dog in an unacceptable manner. Be careful that you don't get into this bad habit.

Should you make the mistake of accidentally reward your dog by picking them up when they are displaying any sort of loud, aggressive or unbalanced energy, you may be silently teaching them to continue with this type of unwanted behaviour and you'll be picking them up even more.

As well, picking up a small dog or puppy when they are barking, growling or acting out in any inappropriate manner, besides being a reward, places them in much more dominant, top dog position where they literally have just gained the higher ground.

Once a dog has gained the literal *"top dog"* position, he or she will feel more confident because they are now looking down on their target and, depending on <u>your</u> energy, will usually then become even more dominant than the person or dog they may have just growled at when they were at "*ground level*".

Rather than accidentally rewarding a dog for displaying unwanted behaviour, a more effective action to take in such a situation is to keep them on the ground, and get their attention back on you. Gently correct your puppy or dog with firm yet calm energy (that is just a little stronger than the energy your dog is displaying) by distracting or interrupting unwanted behaviour with a firm *"No!"* and a quick sideways snap of the leash, which should get them looking to you for direction. This will "tell" your dog that they must let you deal with whatever situation has caused them to react badly.

When the human holding the leash allows a fearful, nervous, shy or bossy dog to deal with situations that unnerve them by growling or cause them to bellow loudly or act out aggressively, the dog's guardian may be unknowingly creating a problem that has the potential to escalate into something very serious.

The same is true of situations where a young puppy may feel the need to protect itself from a larger or older dog that may come charging in for a sniff or is acting confrontational.

It's much easier to prevent unwanted confrontational outbursts between dogs when the human guardian takes responsibility to protect their fur friend, so that the dog never has to feel that they must react out of fear or with aggression in order to protect his or herself or the human at the other end of the leash. While most Labradoodles are usually friendly to unknown dogs, if they are challenged by another more aggressive dog, you don't want your dog to think that you cannot protect them, and that they must now fight back.

No matter the age or size of your puppy or dog, allowing them to display aggression, loud barking or any sort of unwanted behaviour toward another dog, animal or person is NEVER a laughing matter and this type of behaviour must be immediately curtailed.

Excitement Rewards

It's important to recognize that attention paid to an overly excited or out-of-control puppy or dog, even negative attention, is almost certainly going to be rewarding for your fur friend. If your dog is feeling that he or she is not receiving enough of your attention, they are smart enough to quickly learn to do whatever it takes to get the attention they desire.

Bottom line, when you engage with an out-of-control puppy or dog, you are actually rewarding them for acting out in an unstable manner, and inadvertently end up encouraging them to continue with more overly exuberant behaviour you might not be very pleased about.

Many humans make the mistake of accidentally teaching their dogs to act out with crazy energy every time they see them. A good example of this is when humans arrive home and encourage their dog to be excited (more about this below).

Chasing after a puppy when they have taken something they are not supposed to have, picking them up when they're barking or showing aggression, pushing them off when they jump on you or other people, or yelling when they refuse to come when called, can all be forms of negative attention that can be rewarding to your dog and encourage more of the same unwanted behaviour.

Instead, remain calm and consistently firm with your training, so that your dog learns how to control their energy and play appropriately without jumping on everyone or engaging in growling, barking or mouthy behaviour.

Interaction Rewards

If your Labradoodle displays excited energy simply from being petted by you, or anyone else, you will need to teach yourself, your family and your friends to ignore your fur friend until he or she calms down. To do otherwise means that you will be literally teaching your dog that the touch of humans means excitement, and this behavioural problem will continue to escalate.

For instance, when you continue to interact with an overly excited puppy or dog, you are actually rewarding them for out-of-control behaviour and essentially teaching them that when they see humans, you agree with them displaying excited energy.

Too many people encourage their dog to be nuts, for instance, when they return home and greet their dog in a highly excited state. While it's nice to know that your dog is happy to see you, when you forget about being your dog's calm pack leader just a few times, this may be enough to send your smart dog three confusing messages: (1) that they can no longer rely upon you to be their calm leader; (2) that leadership may now be their responsibility; and (3) that seeing humans means they must display out-of-control excitement.

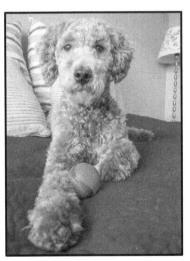

Instead, when you come home, greet your dog calmly and quietly, and if they are at all excited, do NOT touch or speak to them until they calm down. Otherwise, your dog will soon learn that humans are a source of excitement and confusing messages, and long, consistently vigilant work on your part (with help from your friends and family) may be the only way to reverse this chaotic behaviour.

Another thing to keep in mind is that children are often a source of high energy and excitement that can cause a puppy or dog to quickly become extremely wound up. When you wind up a large and bouncy dog, even a friendly one like the Labradoodle, accidents can happen. Young children and unstable seniors can get knocked off their feet, or someone can get scratched if an excited dog jumps up.

If you don't want to create an on-going behavioural problem, that could accidentally get someone injured, you will need to be very vigilant about NOT permitting young children to engage with an excited puppy or dog.

Important Basic Rules and Boundaries

You can prevent many future behavioural problems when you take the time to ensure that your chosen dog learns basic rules and boundaries. All that's necessary for effectively teaching your puppy (or dog) these basics is a calm and consistent approach, combined with your endless patience.

Basic rules and boundaries would include things such as:

- no barking at every little noise
- no barking excessively when someone knocks on the door
- no dogs allowed in the kitchen when preparing food
- no begging at the human's dinner table
- no stealing food from the countertop
- humans through the door first
- no sleeping in the human bed
- no raiding the garbage can
- no jumping up on tables or counters
- no jumping on humans
- no helping yourself to "tootsie rolls" from the cat's litter box
- no chasing the neighbour's cat
- no random digging in the flower bed

Many puppies are ready to begin basic training at about 10 to 12 weeks of age, and some will be ready at 8 weeks. However, be careful not to overdo it when they are less than four months of age, as their attention span may be short. Better to have several short sessions throughout the day.

With younger puppies, make your training sessions no more than 5 or 10 minutes, positive and pleasant with plenty of happy praise and/or treats, so that your puppy will be looking forward to their next session.

Also, begin to introduce hand signals that go along with the verbal commands right away, so that once they learn both, you can remove the verbal commands in favour of just hand signals.

When you teach a dog hand signals, they will become much more attentive because they must look at you to see what you require them to do.

Consistently teach your puppy or dog the ***All Important Three***, which are the "Come", "Sit" and "Stay" commands (more about this in Chapter 12: Training Basics For a Happy Labradoodle), and use them every day in every opportunity to help your young dog progress through their unpredictable adolescent period.

Adolescent Craziness

Too often, we humans become frustrated and impatient and give up on our dogs when they transition from being the cute, cuddly and mostly obedient little puppy they once were and pass into adolescence when they seem to have become all kinds of craziness.

It can often be during this confusing and trying adolescent stage of a dog's life that a once happy and beloved puppy ends up behind bars when the humans who promised to love and protect them, abandon their fur friend at the local SPCA or rescue facility.

With consistency, understanding, the right information, and endless patience and perseverance, you and your fur friend can emerge out the other side of this adolescent period with a much stronger bond.

Firstly, you need to know that not all dogs go through an intensely crazy adolescent period. Secondly, when you remain consistent with your socialising and training during this time, you can live through puppy adolescence and come out the other side a much more knowledgeable and patient guardian.

Remember, you've already lived through potty training, teething, socialising and basic rules and boundaries with your young dog, and you need to feel proud of all your accomplishments and the leaps and bounds you and your puppy have accomplished together over the last several months.

If your adolescent dog is now beginning to act out and push too many of your buttons, rather than giving up on them, it's time to remain calm, consistent and <u>persistent</u>, and re-visit basic rules and boundaries, while keeping in mind that you will eventually be able to enjoy the happy rewards that all those months of diligent puppy training have brought to your relationship.

During adolescence, you may experience several changes in your dog's personality that you're not exactly pleased about. For instance, your young dog may:

- no longer be as friendly with strangers

- begin to show their aggressive side to other dogs

- start to be possessive of their human

- start to bark at unknown people and dogs

- begin to excavate the back yard

- become possessive of toys or their food bowl

- look for opportunities to chase the neighbour's cat

- start to show their stubborn side

- ignore you when called

- begin to chase small creatures

- appear to have suddenly gone deaf

- ignore the basic commands they've already learned

- start to relieve themselves inside again

- bark or whine when left alone

- begin to mark territory

- try to escape the back yard

Welcome to the world of canine adolescence, where it appears that all your previous work has flown out the window and your puppy has turned into some sort of untrustworthy monster.

DON'T PANIC, because every dog is different and your dog's adolescent period may pass by without notice. However, being prepared for the worst will help you ride any possible storm and get you both safely out the other side where you can enjoy an even closer relationship than you previously had.

The most important thing to keep on top of during the adolescent stage in a young dog's life is signs of any sort of aggression. If your dog is beginning

to show their aggressive side to other dogs or people, this must be **immediately** addressed, so that it does not become a very worrisome problem. Use that Martingale collar and leash combination, and any time your young dog growls or tries to lunge at another unknown dog, give a sharp snap toward you and a loud and firm **"NO!"**. Your dog always needs to understand that YOU are in charge, not them.

The adolescent phase may be very subtle for your puppy, or it may be so dramatic that frustration with your fur friend is becoming a daily occurrence and you're questioning whether you made the right choice to invite a dog into your life.

If frustration is getting the upper hand, rather than letting it wear on your last nerve, consider the benefits of hiring a professional, who can provide insight and valuable assistance to help you through this stage of your puppy's development.

Less Obvious Human Mistakes

There are many not so obvious mistakes we humans can inadvertently make when sharing our lives with a dog that can also lead to behavioural problems later in life, some of which include:

Sleeping in Your Bed: many people make the mistake of allowing an adorable crying puppy to sleep with them in their bed. While this may help to calm and comfort a new puppy, it also may set a precedent that could result in behavioural problems later in their life. As well, a sleeping human body could easily crush a small puppy.

As much as it may pull on your heart strings to hear your new puppy crying the first couple of nights in their kennel, a little tough love at the beginning will keep them safe while helping them to learn to both love _and_ respect you as their leader.

FACT *Be aware that it's perfectly fine and natural for your puppy or dog to sleep in the same room with you. After all, they are part of your "pack" and need to be near. Just make sure that you don't let him or her take over YOUR bed.*

Picking Them Up at the Wrong Time: never pick your puppy up if they are displaying aggression (such as growling), fear or nervousness toward an object, other pet or person, because this amounts to rewarding them for displaying unbalanced behaviour.

Instead, your puppy needs to be gently corrected by you, with firm and calm energy, so that they learn to trust your lead and not react out of fear or aggression.

Armpit Alligators: when your dog is a small puppy, be aware that many humans get into the bad habit of carrying a small dog or puppy far too much.

Remember that they need to be on the ground and walking on their own, so that they are not being placed in the leadership position and do not become overly confident. A dog that is carried by their guardian is literally being placed in the _"top dog"_ position.

Be aware that those who constantly carry small dogs or puppies, rather than allowing them to walk on their own, can often accidentally create what I refer to as an _"armpit alligator"_ situation. This is where you see someone carrying a cute little dog that thinks they are the boss of everyone and you stop to say hello, only to be greeted by snapping jaws and sharp teeth.

Even friendly dogs that are usually polite and not naturally wary or suspicious of strangers can learn to become intolerant if they don't receive adequate socialisation. You never want to give your dog the impression that they must protect or be possessive of their humans.

Playing Too Hard or Too Long: many humans play too hard or allow their children to play too long or too roughly with their puppy. You need to remember that your young puppy tires very easily and it's important that they get their rest, especially during the critical growing phases of their young life.

Hand Play: always discourage a puppy from chewing or biting your hands, or any part of your body for that matter.

Do NOT get into the habit of playing the *"hand"* game, where you rough up your puppy and slide them across the floor with your hands. While this may be fun for the puppy and entertaining for the humans, this type of interaction will teach them that your hands are playthings and you will have to work long and hard to break this bad habit.

PERSONAL EXPERIENCE: When my puppy came home with me at 10-weeks of age, the breeder had already been playing the hand game and it took me a very long time to teach my Boris that biting human hands was not acceptable behaviour. Interestingly, when he greets people that he has not seen for years, that he used to know when he was a young puppy, this old habit of play biting hands often re-surfaces for a short while.

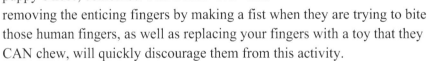

When your puppy is teething, they will naturally need to chew on everything within reach, and this will include you. As cute as you might think it is, this is not an acceptable behaviour and you need to gently, but firmly, discourage the habit.

A light flick with a finger on the end of your puppy's nose, combined with a firm "NO" and removing the enticing fingers by making a fist when they are trying to bite those human fingers, as well as replacing your fingers with a toy that they CAN chew, will quickly discourage them from this activity.

Not Getting Used to Grooming: many people don't realize how important it is to take the time to get their puppy used to a regular grooming routine, including bathing, brushing, clipping, toenail shortening and teeth brushing. When you do not take the time to introduce these important grooming steps early on, this can lead to a lifetime of trauma for both human and dog every time these essential procedures must be performed.

NOTE: get your puppy used to being up high on a table or countertop when it's grooming time. This way, when they must accept a coat clipping session that takes much longer, or a visit to the vet's office, where they will be placed on an examination table, they will not be stressed because this will already be a familiar situation.

Free Feeding: means to always keep food in your puppy's bowl 24/7, so that they can eat any time of the day or night, whenever they feel like it.

While free feeding a young puppy might be a good idea (especially with very small dogs), until they are about four or five months old, many guardians often get into the bad habit of allowing their adult dogs to continue to eat food any time they want, by leaving food out 24/7.

The Labradoodle is a mix of two dogs that are both highly food motivated, which means if there is food out, a Labradoodle will probably eat it. However, while every dog is different, you don't want to get into the habit of leaving food out 24/7 because (a) they will no longer associate you being in control of the food, and (b) if your particular dog gets used to eating too much, they will quickly gain weight and become obese, which can lead to health issues that may shorten their life.

Getting into a free feeding habit can be a serious mistake, as your dog is not a cat, and he or she needs to know that you are firmly in control of their food. Food is a very powerful motivator for dogs, and you being clearly in control of the food will help to establish you as a powerful leader in your dog's mind.

Treating Them Like Children: you do not want to get into the bad habit of treating your dog like a small, furry human. Despite the fact that he or she will usually try their best to please you and their doggy smarts could help them to succeed in most instances, not honouring them for being an amazing dog may cause confusion that could lead to future behavioural problems.

A well-balanced dog thrives when they have a leader that teaches them rules and boundaries. When a dog has a consistently strong human leader, they can relax because they will understand that there is no question that you are their leader and they are your follower. A dog that is not faced with having to make complicated human decisions can live a contented, stress-free life.

Distraction and Replacement: puppies need to be taught what IS and what is NOT acceptable behaviour. For instance, when your puppy tries to chew on your hand, foot, clothing, or anything else that is not fair game, you need to firmly and calmly tell them "NO", and then distract them by replacing what they are not supposed to be chewing with something they are permitted to chew, such as an appropriate toy.

Make sure that you happily praise your puppy every time they make the right choice and choose the toy to chew on. If they persist in chewing on you, remove yourself from the equation by getting up and walking away. If they are really persistent, calmly place them inside their kennel with a favourite chew toy until they calm down.

Always praise your puppy when they discontinue inappropriate behaviour or replace their behaviour with something that is acceptable to you, so that they begin to understand what they can and cannot do. The Labradoodle is a highly intelligent dog that will be eager to please, so this should not be difficult to accomplish.

Flat Collar Nightmares

Many humans simply don't realize how important it is to choose the "right" kind of collar for their canine companion. Also, since there is an ever-increasing array of tempting colours and collar styles to choose from, it's very easy to get distracted  and forget about choosing what is most appropriate for your dog.

What's most important when choosing a collar for your fur friend is picking one that will also keep your dog safe and secure. While the flat collar may be fine for a calm dog that never pulls, leaps about or suddenly tries to do an about face and take off running in a different direction to chase that teasing squirrel or the neighbour's cat, this is not a very safe reality.

 After 40 some years of working with dogs and experiencing possibly every type of terrifying, unexpected disaster while out walking a dog, the ONLY collar I feel absolutely confident using (because I know that the dog I'm in control of cannot wiggle out of it), is the "Martingale" collar.

Flat collars, unless you have them cinched up so tight that you're almost cutting off your dog's air supply, can be fairly easy for most dogs to get out of.

All dogs, no matter their size, are amazing athletes, and even though you may have a firm grip on that leash, they can suddenly become an amazing Houdini, back away from you, wiggle, twist and contort themselves in a quick instant, flip their head and the collar is off – bye, bye doggy!

The Martingale Collar

There are several reasons why the Martingale dog collar **(see photo below)** is far superior to a flat collar, including that:

- 🐾 it's comfortable for your dog to wear all day long

- 🐾 it's safe because your dog cannot wiggle out of it

- 🐾 it's the best training collar

While the Martingale collar looks much the same as a flat collar, there is one very important difference – there is a triangular piece of sliding chain in the middle of it. This chain is attached to the collar with two rings, with a third ring in the middle of the chain, where you attach your leash.

When there is no tension on the collar (from a dog pulling on the leash), the collar hangs loose and comfortable. However, when there IS tension on the collar, that little piece of chain tightens so that your dog cannot get out of their collar.

PERSONAL EXPERIENCE: My dog Boris, despite his short nose, wore the same Martingale "training" collar for almost 15 years. This collar conveys important messages between dog and human.

That little piece of triangular chain makes a slight noise when you sharply tug or jiggle it, and this sends a message to your dog that you want their attention on you. It's simply the best collar for teaching your dog to walk calmly by your side and to remind them that YOU are in charge.

When purchasing a Martingale collar for your dog, take him or her with you because it needs to be the correct size to fit over the widest part of their head. Then, once you've found the right size for your dog, you need to pay strict attention to the <u>correct way to</u> <u>adjust</u> the collar for maximum effect and safety.

FACT *While you can purchase Martingale collars that attach with a plastic clip (rather than going over the head), if you have a large and very strong dog, this type may not be as safe, because a plastic clip can break should a strong dog decide to lunge or pull.*

Adjusting the Martingale Collar: once you've placed the collar over your dog's head, it's important to properly adjust it. First, attach your leash to the outside ring and then adjust the length of the collar so that when you pull it tight and the two inside rings come together, there is still a gap between these two inside rings of approximately two human finger widths. You never want the two inside rings to touch.

You can now enjoy comfortable and safe walks with your happy Labradoodle companion.

Flexi-Leash Fiasco

After much experience with flexi, retractable or extendable dog leashes **(see photo below)** these types of leashes are high on my list of pet peeves for several important reasons, including that they:

- ❧ are dangerous for human and dog alike

- ❧ allow the dog to be in the wrong walking position

- allow the humans to forget their responsibilities

- are heavy, clumsy and difficult to securely grip

- can be an excuse for not properly training your dog

- can accidentally break

- can cause nasty rope burns

- can get dogs and humans tangled up

- can cause fights between dogs

While many people believe that a retractable leash is a good way to allow their dogs more freedom to roam while still keeping them securely attached, the above reasons highlight why these leashes can be a very questionable choice. See below for more details.

Injury to human and dog: these leashes are usually spring-loaded, many feet long (usually 26 feet or 7.9 meters). The thin cords are wound up inside a cumbersome plastic compartment with a handle and a button to control how much of the leash is extended.

As you can imagine, it's far more difficult to control a dog that is roaming about 20 or more feet (6 or more metres) away from you, than it would be if they so much closer, on a standard 4 to 6 foot (1.2 to 1.8 metre) leash and walking at your side.

If your dog gets used to having a roaming distance of 20 feet (6 meters) or more, they will soon forget about you and instead busy themselves with sniffing interesting scents, or run out into traffic. They can be surprised by another dog rushing in, or get tangled up with a person and a dog, which can cause both injury to the dogs and people, or may cause a fight between the two dogs that are tangled up together.

Flexi-leashes can also be serious tripping hazards that can cause many injuries.

MEMORY LANE: The daughter of one of my dog whispering clients broke her toe as a result of tripping over a flexi-leash. I have suffered painful "rope" burns several times, and once was hit in the head (ouch!) with the hard and heavy plastic handle as it snapped back when the young person holding it lost their grip and dropped it.

Further, every flexi or retractable leash is equipped with a brake, designed to stop the unwinding of the cord at various lengths. If your dog is running and all of a sudden comes to the end of their freedom, unless you drop the handle, they will be forced to come to a very abrupt stop that can injure a dog's spine or neck.

Incorrect Walking Position: the ONLY place your dog should ever be when you're out walking with him or her on leash, is beside you, and when you allow them to freely roam 20 or more feet (6 metres) from wherever you are, besides being lax about teaching your dog the correct walking position, you are *"telling"* them that you are no longer in charge.

A dog that is no longer following their human's directions, and believes that leadership has defaulted to him or her, can get you BOTH into a lot of trouble.

Forgetting Your Human Responsibilities: when you're out walking with your puppy or dog, as their leader, you are responsible for everything they do, which includes picking up after them. A retractable leash is long enough to allow your dog to be out of your immediate sight. For instance, while you're busy chatting with a neighbour or checking your phone messages, you may be unaware of what sort of *"message"* your dog may be depositing in the neighbour's yard.

You can be fined for not picking up after your dog, not to mention gaining yourself a bad reputation from your annoyed neighbours, passers-by or other more responsible dog walkers.

Difficult to Securely Grip: the flexi-leash has a large, cumbersome, plastic handle that is quite slippery and difficult to securely hold onto. If your furry companion suddenly lunges or changes direction, the possibility of you losing your grip is quite high, and when that happens, the consequences can be dangerously grave.

Once dropped, your dog is now dragging a bouncing, loudly clattering plastic handle that can be very noisy when being dragged along a sidewalk or other type of hard surface.

MEMORY LANE: This very thing has happened to me in a busy, high traffic area, when walking someone else's dog. While I was lucky and managed to get him safely back, I can tell you from first-hand experience that this is a highly stressful and frightening situation I would not want to wish on anyone.

Unless your dog has been trained to remain calmly sitting at your side while rifles are fired near their head, this loudly clattering flexi leash handle, that seems to be chasing them, can be a very scary experience that will cause most dogs to run fast.

When your dog is scared, they will run even faster, while you run after them adding to the chaos with your panic-stricken screams to stop before they get killed trying to cross a busy intersection. Not a happy scene.

Poor Training: while many might believe they are giving their dog the luxury of more freedom by choosing a retractable leash, they are actually missing out on properly training their dog to heel beside them in the correct walking position.

The very nature of a flexi-leash is such that the dog is often out in front of the person who is supposed to be in charge. When your dog is in front of you, (a) the dog is now in charge; and (b) depending on the temperament of an approaching dog, this may look like a dominant posture, which may result in the other dog believing that he or she must retaliate with aggression. All of this, as you can imagine, has the potential to result in an unpleasant scuffle between dogs and humans.

Accidental Breakage: there is a great deal of wear on a small diameter cord that is constantly unwinding and rewinding and you may not notice a worn area until it actually breaks. If this cord breaks, you've now got a potential runaway dog disaster to hopefully recover from, before the dog gets severely injured, killed by a vehicle, or ends up in some other type of serious trouble.

Improve your training, have better control, make your life easier, avoid injuries, and ensure the safety and security of yourself and your furry best friend by choosing a secure Martingale collar and a standard 4-foot leash.

Sled Dog Fiasco

One last thought about what I call the *"Sled Dog Fiasco"*. Many people think that buying a harness for their dog is a better choice than the proper collar for their canine companion.

However, in almost every circumstance, the only time a harness is actually the right choice is if you have a Springer for your bicycle or a dog-powered scooter, or a strong sled dog that you need to put in harness, so that they can pull you.

While a harness may sometimes be helpful, as a regular walking arrangement, there are many reasons why this may not be the best choice.

What happens when you put most dogs in a harness is that (1) they can no longer see you, because they are automatically in the wrong walking position, being head and shoulders in front of you; (2) you no longer have control of their head and cannot correct unwanted behaviour; (3) they now are your leader and are much more powerful and potentially difficult to control, because the entire weight and strength of their body is attached to that harness; and (4) when the dog is in front of their human, they are seen by other dogs as being the boss, which can cause a more dominant dog to approach in an aggressive manner.

Take Away Tip: "Unless you have a dog powered scooter or a Springer for your bicycle, harnesses are for sled dogs".

In a Nutshell

It cannot be emphasized strongly enough how important it is to properly socialise your puppy so that they will calmly and safely follow your lead in all circumstances. Consider that we humans may often unknowingly reward

our dogs at the wrong time, and that this means that we may be the cause of creating behavioural issues later in life.

Re-visit the information contained in this Chapter and think about what other mistakes you may be accidentally making, so that you can do your best to avoid simple mistakes that can lead to an unhappy dog that suffers from behavioural problems later in life.

Also, when training your dog, keep in mind that the type of leash and collar you choose can make a very big difference.

Chapter 11: Happy Labradoodle Body Language

"Money can buy a fine dog, but
only love can make him wag his tail."
— Kinky Friedman

We all know good communication is not just about the words we use. It's also our energy, tone of voice, our body language that help to package up and deliver our meaning every day.

While most people can effectively communicate their thoughts and feelings through words, with respect to our dogs, we need to generally be reliant upon reading their body language in order to know if they are happy, sad, nervous, afraid or possibly aggressive.

Since our dogs don't speak our spoken language, even though they can certainly learn the meaning of many human words, the only way for us to effectively communicate with them is to understand and recognize what they are telling us through their body language and the vocal sounds they make.

Often, gestures or actions that we assume mean one thing can be the dog telling us the exact opposite. This means that determining what that wagging tail or barking really means can sometimes be the difference between a belly rub and a bite.

How happy would you be if you could not communicate with your family at home? Would you develop behaviour issues over time? Of course, you would, and the same is also true for the canine members of your family.

In order for them to be a happy family member, they need you to understand what they are *"telling you"* and how they feel. For instance, learning to properly "read" your dog's intentions or the intentions of an unknown dog can easily prevent an unwanted encounter during a visit to the local dog park.

Therefore, taking the time to educate yourself about basic canine body language and paying attention to your dog's particular body language (including their face, posture, barking and tail position) can be a valuable skill when raising a content and well-behaved dog.

This Chapter will teach you the basics of exactly that – to understand the what your furry friend (and those dogs around you) are trying to *"tell"* you and how they feel, so that you can share a happy lifelong partnership together.

So, don't wait because now is a good time to begin developing and honing your canine body language skills.

What's With All the Wagging and Barking?

While a well-socialised Labradoodle may often happily wag their tail, it can be a mistake to automatically assume that if your dog, or someone else's dog is wagging their tail, that they are friendly and happy to greet you.

What Does the Wag Mean?

When determining a dog's true intent or temperament, it's important to take into consideration the complete dog posture, rather than just the tail. This is because it's entirely possible that a dog can be wagging his or her tail just before it decides to take an aggressive lunge toward you or your dog.

More important in determining the emotional state of most dogs is the height or positioning of their tail. For instance, a tail that is held parallel to your dog's back usually suggests that they are feeling relaxed, whereas if the tail is held stiffly vertical, this usually means that they may be feeling aggressive, dominant, or highly excited.

Also keep in mind that certain dog tails are carried differently for different reasons. Depending on <u>which</u> dog tail, you will have more or less visible cues. The opposite is also true of other dogs reading your dog's body language.

For instance, a dog with a docked or tightly curled tail (some terriers, Boxers, Bulldogs) can sometimes send confusing messages to others.

A tail held much lower can mean that your dog is feeling stressed, afraid, submissive or unwell and if the tail is tucked underneath the dog's body, this is most often a sign that the dog is feeling highly stressed, nervous, fearful or threatened by another dog, person or unfamiliar situation. If you persist in getting too close to a dog that has their tail tucked, you or your dog may be in for a bite.

When you pay attention to your dog's tail (and any dog tails around you), this can help you to know when you need to step in between and create some space between your dog and another more dominant or nervous dog that is feeling overwhelmed.

Remember that different breeds naturally carry their tails at different heights. Some dogs have tails that curl over the back, or have short or docked tails, while others may not have any visible tail at all. You will need to take this into consideration so that you get used to their particular body language signals.

As well, the speed at which a dog's tail is moving will give you an idea of their mental state because the speed of the wag usually indicates how excited a dog may be.

For instance, a slow, slightly swinging wag can often mean that a dog is tentative or a little nervous about greeting another dog, and this is more of a questioning type of wag, whereas a fast-moving tail held high can mean that a dog is about to challenge or threaten another less dominant dog.

Also, a stalking stance, where a dog has raised hackles (hair along the back), lowers their head, crouches and slowly creeps forward with an intense stare often happens just before a serious attack. There is also a similar-looking *"play"* stance, and without practice, you may have difficulty identifying the difference between the two.

MEMORY LANE: I've been sworn at after politely letting a guardian of a larger dog, who was unaware (and didn't want to know) that their dog was stalking my smaller dog and about to do him harm, so be careful how you approach these situations because some people are unwilling to take any sort of constructive criticism, even though it may have just saved them from a lawsuit.

What Does the Bark Mean?

Of course, our dogs bark for many different reasons, and every dog is different, depending upon their natural breed tendencies and how they were raised. For instance, while many people believe that all small dogs are natural barkers, this is totally false. Even a dog that may have a natural tendency toward barking can be taught to be quiet. In the case of the Labradoodle, barking may occur when bored and stressed from being left alone or in excited anticipation of a walk or a game of fetch. Also, this dog may be an alert watchdog, and without proper training at an early age, may learn to bark more than you might appreciate. This section discusses some of the more common reasons why a dog might be barking.

Communication: since the very first dog, they have communicated with each other over long distances by howling and when in closer proximity, barking or growling to warn off other dogs approaching what they consider to be their territory, or yipping in excitement or happiness when greeting another returning member of their dog pack.

Our domesticated dogs have learned to bark for many of reasons, such as when they sense danger or are alerting us to an unknown person approaching the home.

A dog will also bark in anticipation of their favourite food or game, when they're afraid, frustrated, bored, excited, or to let us know they want to play. Barking is an effective way to get the attention of us humans because no matter the size of the dog, it's a loud and difficult noise to ignore.

Danger: many dogs will bark to alert us to visitors or intruders, and we need to learn how to understand the difference between what our dogs perceive as danger and what is truly dangerous, and indeed how to teach our best friends the difference.

Certainly, we want our dogs to tell us when there is real, imminent danger and should the danger involve an unwanted intruder, we want them to bark loudly to possibly scare this threat away.

However, when our dogs are barking for a reason we're not yet aware of, we need to calmly assess the situation, rather than immediately becoming annoyed or yelling at them to shut up, because they're only trying to tell us something.

We also need to remember that a dog's ability to read energy and body language, plus their sense of smell, hearing and eyesight may be far more acute than our own. This means that we need to give them an opportunity to tell us if they just heard, saw or sensed something worrisome that we need to be aware of.

While any dog can learn to be a big barker, all dogs are unique, and much depends on how they were raised. If your dog seems to be overly eager to bark at everything, you will need to take the time to teach him or her when to stop.

Rather than ignoring our dogs (or yelling at them) when they are attempting to *"tell"* us that something is bothering them, even if we ourselves understand that the noise the dog just heard is only the neighbor's kids coming home from school or a postal delivery, we need to respond appropriately.

We need to calmly acknowledge our dog's concern by saying, *"OK, good dog,"* and then ask them to come to you. This way you have quietly and calmly let your dog know that the situation is nothing to be concerned about and you have asked them to move away from the target they are concerned about, which places you in control, and which will usually stop the barking.

Often when a dog doesn't understand what a particular noise is, because they can't see it, it's only natural for them to bark. If you just show them what caused the particular noise, they will then learn that it is nothing to be concerned about, and perhaps the next time they hear the same noise, they will know that it is nothing to bark about.

Attention: many dogs will learn to bark to get their owner's attention, just because they are bored, need some exercise, or want to be taken outside for an interesting walk or a trip to the local park to chase a ball.

Our canine companions are very good at getting us to do their bidding, and if we fall for it, we can be teaching our dog to be bossy and setting ourselves up for an annoying precedent that could plague us for the remainder of our relationship.

MEMORY LANE: I shared my life with a Blue Heeler who would go berserk with loud barking every time we drove near a park or when we arrived at a park. Even so, I would never reward him for barking, because as annoying and hard on the eardrums as it was, I had to sit calmly inside the vehicle until he stopped barking. If I had let him immediately bound out of the vehicle, I would have inadvertently taught my dog that barking got him exactly what he wanted.

When a dog is barking to gain their guardian's attention (unless they are in distress), before we immediately capitulate, first we need to calmly ask our dog to make eye contact with us, and do something we ask of them. After our dog has performed a calm and quiet task for us, such as sit or lie down, then we can decide to give our dog our undivided attention on our terms.

 If you're having difficulties teaching your dog to cease and desist from too much barking, often teaching them to bark on command (with a hand signal) will solve the problem. Once a dog learns to bark with a hand signal, they will often stop the random barking, because they will be waiting for you to ask them to bark.

Doggy Swearing: Often you will see a dog and their guardian at the local dog park playing fetch and when the human is not throwing that ball quickly enough to satisfy the dog's manic desire to run and fetch, the dog will be madly barking at their guardian. This is the equivalent of being sworn at in doggy language.

Be careful that you're not making the mistake of allowing your puppy or dog to manipulate you in this type of situation, because if you do, you will soon create a habit that will very quickly become not just annoying or embarrassing to you, but also irritating to everyone else at the park.

Before throwing a ball or Frisbee for a dog that loves to chase and retrieve (like the Labradoodle), it's important to slow it down and always ask the dog to first sit or lay down and make eye contact with you.

Often the types of canines that are overly exuberant with chasing a ball or Frisbee have learned this annoying barking behaviour from their humans, who allowed themselves to be literally at the beck and call of their dog, and accidentally created this noisy habit by immediately throwing the ball every time the dog barked. Think about it – dog barks, human throws ball – who's in charge here?

In this situation, if you allow your dog to dictate to you when you will throw the ball, it will take no time at all for them to learn that barking gets them their desired result, and you may have just created an annoying, rude dog who is yelling at you in doggy language to do their bidding.

In this type of ball-retrieving scenario, the dog has become ball *"obsessed"* and is no longer really paying attention to you or your commands, because they are solely focusing on where the ball is.

While there are many situations in which your dog may bark to convey that they've heard a noise, in all other situations where the barking is demanding an action, attention, a toy, other object or food, this is when you need to ask them to do something for you, and then only if you want to give them what they are asking for, do you follow through.

MEMORY LANE: I once had a client whose dog would start to loudly bark and howl every time he answered the phone. As you can imagine, this was big time annoying because nobody could hear what was being said. After a quick dog whispering session, this noisy canine companion quickly learned that this was not acceptable behaviour and the problem was solved.

Bottom line, remember to stay calm when your cute puppy is demanding attention, because even negative attention can be rewarding for your dog, and can lead down a future, unwanted path where he or she will learn further habits that will not be particularly endearing for the human side of the relationship once the cute puppy has become an adult.

Boredom or Separation Anxiety: many dogs, especially those who have not been properly trained, are treated like children, are under-exercised, or that have not been taught firm rules and boundaries, will sharply bark when left at home and are bored or are feeling the anxiety of being separated from their humans.

`reminder` ***Many times, we humans believe that our dog is barking when being left alone, because he or she is experiencing "separation anxiety", when in fact what the dog is really experiencing is the frustration of observing a member of the pack which they believe to be their follower (i.e., You) leaving them.***

This can happen if a guardian is not a strong enough leader for their smart Labradoodle and he or she has taken over. They may then loudly verbalize their frustration and displeasure because, in the dog world, the pack follower (which the human in the relationship may have allowed themself to become) does NOT leave the pack leader (them). *I've seen this type of situation many times over, and once the human side of the relationship becomes a stronger leader and takes control, it quickly reverses.*

Breaking your dog of the habit of loud barking when they are left alone can be solved in different ways, with the most obvious being that you simply

take your dog with you wherever you go. After all, they are pack animals, and in order for them to be really happy and well balanced, they need the constant direction of their leader (which is supposed to be you).

Another much more time-consuming way to solve a barking problem, could involve hiring a professional to help assess why the problem has occurred in the first place and then devise an effective plan to reverse the problem that will work for each unique situation.

Fear or Pain: another reason your dog may bark is when they are feeling frightened or in pain and this is usually a type of bark that sounds quite different from all the others, often being a combination of a bark and a whine, or a yelping type of noise.

This is a bark that you will want to pay close attention to, so that you can quickly respond and offer the assistance that your puppy or dog may need.

Whatever the reason your dog may be barking, always remember that this is how they communicate and *"tell"* us that they want something or are concerned, afraid, nervous or unhappy about something, and as their guardians, we humans need to pay attention.

Raised Hackles: when your dog approaches with raised hackles (the hair along the dog's back), while this can be an indication that the dog may be approaching with dominant or aggressive tendencies, it also may be an indication that he or she is excited, fearful, startled, anxious or lacks confidence.

In any of these circumstances (whether it's your dog or someone else's), it's a good idea to be respectful and keep your distance until you can assess what's really going on. A dog that is feeling nervous, anxious or fearful can quickly turn into a reactive biting dog, and I can tell you from personal experience that being bitten by any dog really hurts.

In a Nutshell

Learning your dog's particular body language can take some time, and this Chapter will help you get started. The more you are out and about with your dog, visiting and socialising in local parks and going on walks where you will find other dogs, animals and people to observe, the more opportunity

you will have to become skilled at recognizing the many subtleties of canine body language.

Paying attention to your dog's verbal and body-language signals as explained above, will help you figure out what message they are trying to get across to you or other dogs you may meet, and this can make all the difference in preventing confusion or unwanted encounters for you both while raising a happy and well-behaved dog.

One last thought about body language and energy – check in with your own body language and energy before you walk out the door attached to your dog. This can be more important than you might imagine, because if you're not in the moment and have your mind on something that has nothing to do with enjoying a successful and pleasant walk with your dog, you may be setting yourself up for trouble.

For example, if you go out the door with your dog while displaying sad, weak, fearful, distracted or confusing energy of any sort, your dog will pick up on this and become nervous or confused and wonder if leadership has just defaulted to them. In other words, if <u>your energy</u> is not clearly conveying to your dog that you are in charge, you can literally be the cause of an uncomfortable or aggressive encounter with another person walking their dog.

It's VERY important to keep in mind that when walking with a dog (especially a sturdy and tenacious one that may have a naturally dominant personality to start with), the moment he or she senses you are no longer completely in control of their actions, they will take this unspoken "cue" from you that being in charge has now defaulted to them.

You <u>never</u> want any dog to feel they must protect you from the postman, neighbour's cat or that taunting little Chihuahua walking across the street, because if they do, you're literally out walking with a highly charged, unpredictable, live "weapon" that could decide to go off at any moment.

Most Labradoodles will be polite when out walking, IF you are in charge and IF you have put in the time to properly train and socialise them. This little dog will also not be deterred by their smaller size, and most likely will not back down if they feel challenged by another dog that could be much larger.

Never forget that this tenacious breed was originally a sturdy, determined, working dog that would effectively exterminate rats. Therefore, should you permit your dog to take their prey drive into their own paws and, for instance, terrorize the neighbour's cat, you could end up with a lawsuit on your hands, and/or sky-high veterinary bills if this companion is permitted to be confrontational with another animal, and that's if you're lucky.

While it would usually be a rare occurrence for the Labradoodle to harm a human, the same may not hold true when encountering an unknown dog that approaches with an aggressive or challenging stance.

It's always a good idea to keep in mind that if your dog harms another dog, animal or person, or causes stress to another animal or takes chase with murderous intent, the consequences could be far worse than a high vet bill. For instance, any dog that bites could face a death sentence or a ruling that they can never be seen in public unless they're wearing a muzzle.

Chapter 12: Training Basics for a Happy Labradoodle

*"Everyone thinks they have the best dog
in the world. None of them are wrong."*
— Unknown

It's no surprise that a properly trained dog will be a much happier, safe and more secure companion that everyone enjoys being around, and that will be far less likely to develop behaviour issues later in life.

When your dog respects your leadership and there is no question that YOU are in charge, your dog can then relax and let you take the lead in every situation, which is as it should be.

Developing a basic training program and learning to teach the bright and athletic Labradoodle commands and discipline is all part of establishing yourself as the leader and starting your dog off on the right paw.

Therefore, this Chapter will focus on training basics and tips, including hand signals, as well as simple tricks that your dog will love to learn. Take heed humans, because you will be very glad that you spent the time to learn everything contained in these pages.

All of our canine companions are amazing, natural athletes and because of this, no matter their size or breed, they need humans to lead them and daily mental and physical exercise to keep them fit and healthy, so that they can be happy and well-mannered family members. While this dog is capable of learning much more, part of every dog's exercise routine should include learning at least the three most important training commands, which are **"Come, Sit and Stay"**.

This strong and sturdy dog is a versatile athletic companion that needs vigorous daily activity to prevent them from becoming overweight and mentally unsettled. He or she will love going for hikes, jogging, brisk walks and endless adventures with you. Most of all, these dogs will live for as much vigorous outdoor activity as possible with their guardian, and when well socialised, may also enjoy playing with other known dogs.

A happy and contented Labradoodle needs disciplined exercise every day to prevent the anxiety and frustration that an inactive life can create until it has nowhere to go except to display itself through barking, destructive behaviour or aggression.

If you find that your dog is being a pest by chewing inappropriate items around the home, being demanding of your time, or especially unruly when visitors come to call, this is likely because their mind is not being challenged enough or their body is not being exercised often enough, vigorously enough, or long enough each day to drain out their daily pent-up energy reserves.

A healthy, adult dog will thrive when being walked several times each day and mentally challenged by being engaged in other forms of disciplined canine activity, such as Agility, Flyball, Trick Training, Barn Hunt or even Advanced Obedience.

This is a smart dog so use your imagination and find out what canine sports YOUR dog may enjoy learning. Who knows, maybe he or she will be the next skateboarding dog. So long as you prove to him or her that you mean what you say through firm, fair direction and consistency, rather than too many treats, they will not feel the need to manipulate or question your authority, and will happily follow your direction.

Even at the young age of eight to ten weeks, most dogs are capable of beginning to learn anything you can teach. If you wait until this sturdy dog is six months old before beginning any serious training program, you could already have a determined and stubborn problem on your hands and a wilful dog that may be unwilling to heed your commands.

 The backbone of helping to develop a well-balanced and happy dog is to provide them with a routine that ensures sufficient time to satisfy their particular daily physical and mental exercise needs; that might include a canine sport, plus ensuring they can be with you for the majority of their time, in combination with the opportunity to play, freely run, sniff, search and explore their world every day.

What you can teach this active and agile canine companion depends entirely upon you and the time and patience you have to devote to their education. Never under-estimate what incredible hidden talents your dog may have.

No matter what you decide to teach, always train with firm patience, kindness, consistency and positive rewards.

 Never train with anger or raised voices as this dog may be sensitive, and wants to please and will quickly learn whatever you have the patience to teach.

When all training sessions are happy and fun-filled with plenty of treat rewards and positive reinforcement, your dog will be a happy, attentive student who trusts and respects you as their leader and looks forward to learning new commands, tricks and routines.

Puppy Training Basics

First, choose a *"Discipline Sound"* that every human family member will always use. Being consistent with this warning sound will make it much easier for your puppy to learn what they can or cannot do and will be very useful when redirecting your puppy before they engage in unwanted behaviour.

The best types of sounds are short and sharp, so that the sound will immediately get the attention of your puppy, and make it easy for you to interrupt or redirect them before they make a mistake.

It doesn't really matter what sound you choose, so long as it gets your dog's attention and everyone in the family is consistent with using it. A sound I have found to be very effective with most dogs is a simple *"UH!"* sound that is said sharply and with emphasis.

Most puppies and dogs respond immediately to this sound and when caught in the middle of doing something they're not supposed to be doing, they will quickly stop and look to you for direction, or back away from what they were doing.

Next, your puppy needs to learn the Three Most Important Words, which are **"*Come*"**, **"*Sit*" and "*Stay*"**. These three basic commands will help to keep your puppy safe in almost every circumstance.

For instance, when you teach your puppy the *"Come"* command, they will quickly return to your side should they see danger approaching. Further, every time you teach your puppy or dog commands, you will be further solidifying your leadership role, and a dog that clearly understands that their human guardian is in control will be a safe and happy follower.

Most puppies are ready to begin training at approximately 10 to 12 weeks of age (and some even earlier). You won't want to wait until they are much larger and more difficult to control, especially with a larger dog, like the Labradoodle. When they are still very young make your training sessions no more than 5 or 10 minutes (2 or 3 times a day). Also make sure that all training sessions are positive and pleasant with lots of praise and/or treat rewards so that your puppy will be looking forward to their next session.

To help you understand the big three commands, yours truly demonstrates what the hand signals look like in the following pictures!

COME:

The first and most important command you need to teach your puppy is the recall, or *"Come"* command.

- 🐾 Begin the *"Come"* command inside your home.

- 🐾 Go into a larger room, such as your living room area.

- 🐾 Place your puppy in front of you and attach their leash or a longer line to their Martingale collar, while you back away from them a few feet.

- 🐾 Say the command *"Come"* in an excited, happy voice and hold your arms open wide.

- 🐾 If they do not immediately come to you, gently give a tug on the leash, so that they understand that they are supposed to move toward you.

- 🐾 When they come to you, happily praise them and give a treat they really enjoy.

Once your puppy can accomplish a *"Come"* command flawlessly inside your home, it's then time to graduate them to your back yard, a nearby park or quiet outside area where you will repeat the process and where there will be many more distractions.

In order to keep yourself and your dog safe, he or she needs to always come to you when asked, despite whatever distractions may be nearby.

When you're working with your dog on the "Come" command outside, you may want to purchase an extra-long, lightweight line (25 or 50 feet), so that you are always attached and can encourage them in the right direction should they become distracted by noises, scents and other dogs.

Choose a time of day when there will be fewer distractions when you're beginning this outside training, and remember that swiftly moving objects, dogs or other small creatures may also be a difficult distraction for a Labradoodle with a strong retrieving drive to ignore.

Once your dog always comes running when called, you can practise without the verbal command, and just show them the signal, which they will be able to see from across the park.

Keep in mind that even after teaching your Labradoodle the important *"Come"* command, their nose may take precedence during outdoor teaching sessions if an interesting dog, scent or fast-moving object or creature distracts them. Remember that a puppy's attention span will be much shorter than a grown dog's.

Always keep a young dog on leash when working in an area where they can easily run off in pursuit of any distraction.

SIT:

The **"Sit"** and **"Stay"** commands are both very easy commands to teach that will help to keep your puppy or dog safe and out of harm's way in almost every circumstance. Find a quiet time to teach these commands when your puppy is not overly tired.

- ❧ Ask your puppy to **"Sit"** and if they do not yet understand the command, show them what you mean by gently squeezing with your thumb and middle finger the area across the back that joins with their back legs.

- ❧ NEVER just push them down into a sit, as this can cause damage to their back or joints.

- ❧ When they sit, give them a treat and praise them.

- ❧ When you say the word **"Sit"**, at the same time show them the hand signal for this command.

- ❧ While you can use any hand signal, the universal signal for **"Sit"** is right arm (palm open facing upward) parallel to the floor, and then raising your arm while bending at the elbow toward your right shoulder.

- ❧ Once your dog is sitting reliably for you, remove the verbal "Sit" and replace it with just the hand signal.

Every time you take your dog out for a walk, which is often a cause of excitement, get into the habit of asking them to sit quietly and patiently at every stage of your walk.

For instance, ask your dog to sit and patiently wait while you put on their leash, while you put on your shoes or jacket, after you approach the door, after you are on the other side of the door, while you lock the door, every time you arrive at a street intersection or crosswalk, every time you stop during your walk to speak to a neighbour, greet a friend or admire the view, etc., and practise all this in reverse when heading back home.

When you are consistent with the *"Sit"* training, it will soon become automatic for your dog to calmly sit every time you stop walking without you even asking. ***That's called an "automatic" sit.***

When you ask your dog to sit for you, they are learning several things all at once: (1) that they must calmly pay attention to you; (2) that you are their leader; (3) that they must look at you for direction; and (4) that they must respect you as their leader.

Keep in mind that a sitting puppy or dog is much easier to control than one standing at the alert, ready to bolt out the door or jump up on someone. As well, the action of sitting helps to calm the mind of an excited puppy (or dog), which makes teaching your puppy the *"Sit"* command a very important part of their daily interactions with your family members as well as people you may meet when out on a walk.

When you ask your puppy to *"Sit"* before you interact in any way with them, before you go out, before you feed them, before you remove their leash, etc., you are helping to quiet their mind, while teaching them to look to you for direction, and at the same time making it more difficult for them to jump, lunge or disappear out a door.

STAY:

- Once your puppy can reliably **"Sit"**, firmly say the word **"Stay"** (with authority in your voice) and hold your outstretched arm, palm open toward their head while backing away a few steps.

- If they try to follow, calmly say **"No"** and put them back into "Sit".

- Give a treat and then firmly say again **"Stay"** at the same time as the hand signal and back away a few steps.

- Practise these three basic **"Come"**, **"Sit"**, **"Stay"** commands everywhere you go, and use the **"Sit"** command as much as you can to ensure its success rate.

As your puppy matures, and their attention span increases, you will be able to train for longer periods of time and introduce more complicated routines. This is a smart, alert, thinking dog that wants to please and can easily learn many words and hand signals.

Hand Signals

It's really important to introduce the hand signals that go along with the verbal commands you use during training, so that once your furry student learns both, you can remove the verbal commands in favour of just hand signals. A dog that looks at you for direction, rather than listening to your voice, will be a much more attentive follower.

As well as being a more natural way for your dog to communicate, hand signal training is by far the most useful and efficient training method for any dog.

All too often we inundate our canine companions with a great deal of human chatter and noise that they really don't understand, but because they are so willing to be part of our world, they soon learn the meaning of many words.

Contrary to what some people might think, the first language of every dog has nothing to do with them learning words, but rather is a combination of sensing energy and watching body language, which requires no spoken word or sound.

Therefore, when we humans take the time to teach our dog hand signals for all their basic commands, we're then communicating with them at a level they instinctively understand, plus we're helping them to become focused followers, as they must watch us in order to understand what is required of them.

Simple Tricks

When teaching your dog tricks, in order to give him or her extra incentive, find a treat that they really like and give the treat as a positive reward when they do what you ask, because this will help solidify a good performance.

Most dogs will be extra attentive during training sessions when they anticipate that they will be rewarded with their favourite treats – especially this dog, who will usually have a healthy appetite.

If your puppy is less than six months old when you begin teaching them tricks, while you can train several times a day, keep your sessions short (no more than 5 or 10 minutes) and always fun. As they become adults, you can extend the length of your sessions, as they will be able to maintain their focus for longer periods of time.

SHAKE A PAW:

Who doesn't love a well-trained dog that knows how to shake a paw? This is one of the easiest tricks to teach your dog.

☙ Find a quiet place to practice, without noisy distractions or other pets, and stand or sit in front of your dog.

☙ Place them in the sitting position and have a treat in your left hand.

☙ Say the command **"Shake"** while putting your right hand behind their left or right paw and pulling or tapping the back of the paw gently toward yourself until you are holding their paw in your hand.

☙ Immediately praise them and give their favourite treat.

☙ Most dogs will learn the **"Shake"** trick quite quickly, and very soon, you won't need to use the word at all because once you put out your hand, your dog will immediately lift their paw and put it into your hand, without your assistance or any verbal cue.

Practice every day until they are 100% reliable with this trick, and then it will be time to add another trick to their repertoire.

 Most dogs are naturally either right or left pawed. If you know which paw your dog favours, ask them to shake this paw.

ROLL OVER:

You will find that just as your dog is naturally either right or left pawed, they will also naturally want to roll either to the right or the left side. Take advantage of this by asking your dog to roll to the side they naturally prefer.

- Sit with your dog on the floor and put them in a lie down position.

- Hold a treat in your hand and place it close to their nose without allowing them to grab it.

- While they are in the lying position, move the treat to the right or left side of their head (the nose will follow the treat), so that they have to roll over to get to it. You can help them roll if they seem to be having trouble at first.

- You will very quickly see which side they want to naturally roll to, and once you see this, move the treat to this side.

- When they roll over to this side, immediately give them the treat and praise them.

- You can say the verbal cue **"Over"** while you demonstrate the hand signal motion (moving your right hand in a circular motion) or moving the treat from one side of their head to the other with a half circle motion. Soon you will be able to remove the verbal cue and just use the hand signals.

SIT PRETTY:

While this trick is a little more complicated, and most dogs pick up on it very quickly, remember that every dog is different so always exercise patience.

- Find a quiet space with few distractions and sit or stand in front of your dog and ask them to **"Sit"**.

- Have a treat nearby (on a countertop or table) and when they sit, use both of your hands to lift up their front paws into the sitting pretty position, while saying the command **"Sit Pretty"**.

- Help them balance in this position, while you praise them and give them the treat.

- Once your dog can perform the balancing part of the trick quite easily without your help, sit or stand in front of your dog while asking them to **"Sit Pretty"**.

- Holding the treat above their head at the level of their nose would be when they sit pretty. If they're having trouble balancing, you can place them beside a wall to give them more support when you're first beginning this trick.

- If they attempt to stand on their back legs to get the treat, you may be holding the treat too high, which will encourage them to stand on their back legs to reach it. Go back to the first step and put them back into the **"Sit"** position and again lift their paws while their backside remains on the floor.

- After they learn the trick on verbal command, try saying the verbal cue while demonstrating the hand signal: holding your straight arm, fully extended, over your dog's head with a closed fist (pictured).

- Make this a fun and entertaining time for both of you and practice a few times every day until they can **"Sit Pretty"** just with hand signal command every time you ask.

A smart young puppy, like the Labradoodle, should be able to easily learn these basic tricks before they are six months old and when you are patient and make your training sessions short, fun and rewarding for your dog, they will be eager to learn so much more.

Crate Training

The best method for housetraining your dog is called crate training. Basically, you give your puppy many opportunities to do his or her business outside, so they are not tempted to do it inside.

During times when you cannot keep a constant watch on your puppy (such as when you're taking a shower, making dinner or sleeping), you put him or her in their crate as this will help to prevent hidden accidents elsewhere in your house. As long as you use the crate for this purpose and you help your puppy form a positive association with the crate, he or she will not mind being in it. Just be certain that you never use it as a form of punishment!

So, how exactly do you go about house training your puppy? Here's a step-by-step guide:

1. Choose a certain part of your yard where you want your dog to go.
2. Take your puppy outside every hour or so -- directly to the chosen spot every time.
3. When you take your puppy out, say "Go pee" as soon as you set him or her down in that area.
4. Wait for your puppy to do his business – and the moment they do, immediately praise them in an excited voice and give a small treat as a reward.
5. If your puppy does not have to go, take them back inside instead of letting them wander around. You want them to understand that they are there for a purpose, not just to sniff the flowers.
6. When you're at home, keep a close eye on your puppy and confine them to whatever room you are in.
7. Watch your dog for signs that he or she has to go and take them outside immediately if they start to sniff the ground, walk in circles, act agitated, move toward the door or squat.
8. During times when you cannot physically watch your puppy, put him or her in their crate to reduce the risk of an accident – do not keep any food or water in the crate with them.
9. Let your puppy go outside to relieve his or herself immediately before putting them in the crate and also immediately after releasing them. You should also take your puppy outside shortly after a meal or when they wake up from a nap.
10. Take away your puppy's food and water about an hour before bedtime until they are able to go the whole night without an accident.

When you first bring your puppy home, don't expect him or her to be able to hold their bladder or bowels for more than an hour or two. Even so, you should start crate training right away so they learn good habits from an early age. As they get older, they will be able to wait longer before needing a bathroom break – about one hour for each month of age.

Adult Training

The Labradoodle is a loving, often sensitive dog that will thrive so long as they are getting to spend fun time and activities close to their humans. Therefore, in order to ensure a happy and healthy dog that will not develop behaviour issues out of boredom or laziness, make sure that you get your dog involved in interesting activities, such as Advanced Obedience, Trick Training, Agility, Flyball or perhaps Barn Hunt.

When your dog is a full-grown adult (approximately two years of age), you will definitely want to begin more complicated or advanced training sessions with this smart and energetic fur friend.

When you have the desire and patience, you may be surprised at how many commands, tricks, routines or canine sports you can teach a happy, willing Labradoodle who trusts and respects their human guardian.

For instance, you may wish to teach your adult dog more advanced tricks, such as opposite sided paw shakes or rollovers, which are more difficult than you might think and which this agile and smart dog is definitely capable of learning.

If you and your dog are having fun learning new tricks or routines together, consider teaching him or her a series of hand signals, such as *"Commando crawl"*, *"Speak"* or *"Jump through the human hoop"*, or perhaps get them certified as a therapy dog so they can brighten the days of those who can no longer care for a dog of their own and must spend time in hospitals and care facilities.

Beyond just being a fun thing to do, teaching your dog tricks and routines builds a strong bond of trust and respect, and is a healthy way to exercise both your dog's mind and body, which will result in a happy, contented and well-behaved companion.

Over-Exercising

Be especially careful about over-exercising your fur friend when it's warm outside because like humans, dogs can also collapse from heat stroke. Also, don't over-exercise a young puppy (as their muscles and bones are not yet fully developed).

Playtime

Every dog needs some down time or regular playtime each day when they can enjoy just being a dog. While each dog will be different with respect to what types of games they may enjoy, most will really love any game involving retrieving a fast-moving ball or soft toy. Retrieving will be a favourite pastime for this dog, because retrieving on land and water is in the history of both of their parents.

The loving and very smart Labradoodle may also be a very excited participant in a fun game of *"Search"*, where you ask your dog to *"Sit/Stay"* while you hide a favourite treat that they then have to use their nose to find.

To begin teaching the "Search" game, when they are first learning how the game works, ask your dog to "Sit/Stay" while you slowly back away and place a treat on the floor where they can actually still see it. Return to where they are remaining in their sit/stay and excitedly say, "OK! Search!" and point to where you just placed the treat. Each time you play this game, you can place the treat farther and farther away and then completely out of their sight before you release them to "Search!". Once your dog gets the hang of this game, you can hide the treat anywhere they have to use their nose to find it, such as on the arm of a chair, under a toy, on top of a low ledge or in their dog bed.

After a disciplined walk, a well-socialised dog will also enjoy being given the opportunity for some off-leash freedom to really stretch out by running free to play with other similar-sized dogs at the local dog park.

In a Nutshell

Taking the time to teach your dog the most important three commands, basic rules and boundaries plus simple or complex tricks and interesting tasks and routines or sports that engage the mind, will keep this smart companion both mentally and physically healthy and happy and you will raise a well-behaved dog that is a joy to be around.

The friendly Labradoodle will be an affectionate and gentle family companion with a loyal, loving personality that is eager to please and quick to learn.

Chapter 13: What If You Slip Up?

"Dogs got personality.
Personality goes a long way."
— Quentin Tarantino

All the information, suggestions, tips and advice given in this book is the result of more than 40-years' experience helping humans positively and effectively interact with the canine world.

If you take all that is written on these pages to heart, and regularly and consistently apply what you've learned, your dog will grow up to be a happy family member that will not have to suffer from common behavioural issues.

However, if your energy level is not compatible with this breed, your lifestyle drastically changes, you forget to exercise your dog or keep on top of socialising and rules and boundaries, you let your dog take over, or you slip up for any number of reasons, problems may inevitably occur.

For instance, you may end up becoming too busy or distracted with your human life to provide your canine companion with what he or she needs on a daily basis to be a happy and fulfilled member of your family.

Realistically, there may be any number of reasons why you may not be consistently applying the information provided here, and the following is an outline of just a few of the more common behavioural issues that could occur, with some tips that may help you quickly get back on track.

When reading the following pages, please keep in mind that a specific behavioural problem is usually the result of many different possibilities or

circumstances that have taken place between the human individual or family and the particular dog.

This is why effectively addressing a specific unwanted behaviour so that it can be eliminated often requires the assistance of a professional with a personal approach, and well-honed detective skills, that can ask the right questions to determine how the unwanted behaviour may have initially occurred, because it's often not what you may have initially thought.

Therefore, to generically outline possible ways that could reverse an unwanted behaviour will be a guessing game. In other words, without knowing the circumstances of the guardian and their family and figuring out what may have triggered the unwanted behaviour, I can only make my best guess based on previous experience with similar problems.

As an example, there might be many reasons why the dog in question is, for instance, chewing the tassels on your precious Persian rug. As an example, this could be because they:

- 🐾 are hungry
- 🐾 are teething
- 🐾 have a taste for wool
- 🐾 think the tassels are a toy
- 🐾 are a super high energy dog
- 🐾 are left alone and are frustrated

- ❖ haven't been given appropriate toys to chew

- ❖ have not been taught rules and what is appropriate

- ❖ need a guardian with stronger leadership energy

- ❖ are bored and under-exercised

- ❖ are over-stimulated

As you can imagine, because there are endless dog and human combinations and unique situations, there are almost endless scenarios and reasons why a dog may develop a particular behavioural issue.

Therefore, please understand that without close observation and much detective work, the following few common behavioural problems and the suggestions for alleviating them, will be my best guess.

Chewing Inappropriate Items
[Re-visit "*Distraction and Replacement*" in Chapter 10]

If your puppy or dog is chewing the carpet, your fingers, the legs of the coffee table, the remote, your shoes, or any other inappropriate item(s) that are not dog toys, rather than getting upset with your dog, you need to train yourself to be much more vigilant, and then **distract and replace**.

First make sure that all the chewing is not just because the puppy is teething. We must have compassion during teething, because this is a painful time for the puppy and they must chew to help alleviate the pain while those adult teeth are growing in.

Always make sure your puppy has plenty of chew toys and to help with the teething pain, give your puppy an old T-towel soaked in water, tied in knots and frozen in the freezer as a chew toy.

When your dog is a little older, already has pushed through their adult set of teeth and has decided, for instance, that the legs on your coffee table are good chew toys, it may be possible that you:

- ❖ are not paying attention and taking the time to make sure your dog receives enough vigorous daily exercise, and/or,

❧ are not teaching your dog what is, and what is not appropriate for chewing by saying a firm and convincing "No", replacing the table leg with a toy they <u>are</u> allowed to chew, and praising them when they've got the right thing between their teeth.

Being Fearful of Loud Noises
[Re-visit *"Fear of Loud Noises"* in Chapter 10]

If you have raised a dog that has a fear of loud, popping noises, perhaps you skipped the information in Chapter 10 or forgot to apply the suggestions outlined, so take a moment now to read through this and practice until your dog loses or at least diminishes their fear.

Excessive Excitement When Friends Visit
[Re-visit *"Chapter 3: Overview of the Happy Labradoodle"* and *"Chapter 12: Training Basics for a Happy Labradoodle"*]

Make sure that you begin to teach an excitable young dog to be a calm follower as soon as you bring him or her home.

Always ignore an excited dog and do <u>not</u> touch or speak to them until they are calm and relaxed, otherwise you will literally be inadvertently teaching them that it is acceptable behaviour for them to be excited every time they see a human.

If they are overly excited when friends come to visit, stand between your dog and your friends, and create some space by pointing away and firmly telling your dog, *"GO"*, and also ask your friends to ignore him or her.

Further, if you've been properly training your puppy or dog, you will have taught them to *"Sit"* on command, and a sitting dog is much more relaxed and easier to control.

Acting Aggressively on a Walk
[Re-visit *"Chapter 12: Training Basics for a Happy Labradoodle"*]

Make sure that your dog is wearing the right collar and leash and is walking at your side without pulling when you're out for your walks together.

When you train your dog to walk beside you, this *"tells"* them that YOU are their leader and in charge of every situation, which means they will be much less likely to act out or attempt to "protect" you from outside stimuli. If they DO try, immediately give a sharp tug (toward yourself) on that Martingale collar along with a strong *"NO!"* to interrupt unwanted behaviour and remind them who is the boss.

Pulling When on Leash
[Re-visit *"The Martingale Collar"* in Chapter 10]

If your dog is pulling on leash, chances are high that he or she is not wearing the proper training collar and you may not have taken the time to teach them to quietly walk at your side.

Purchase a Martingale collar for your dog, properly adjust it, and then the next time they try to pull ahead of your left knee, give a sharp snap to this collar (toward yourself) and firmly say the word *"Heel"*.

Repeating this process until your dog understands can take a few minutes or even several days, as each dog is different – be consistent and persistent until your dog gets it.

Also, turning circles or figure eights and changing directions suddenly when on a leash walk will quickly help to teach your dog their proper walking position, because if they are ahead of you, they are going to be stepped on or walked into.

Stealing Food or Raiding the Garbage Can
[Re-visit *"Ideal Living Conditions for a Happy Labradoodle"* in Chapter 6]

The Labradoodle will usually be a highly food motivated breed. This is a sturdy, agile and athletic dog that will have no difficulty jumping up on counter tops. If given the opportunity and the food is enticing enough, any dog will steal food. This means that in order to avoid this possibility, you must be a vigilant guardian and make sure that you never leave any food they should not eat unattended or where they can reach it.

Not Obeying Commands
[Re-visit *"Chapter 12: Training Basics for a Happy Labradoodle"*]

A well-trained Labradoodle is one that obeys the basic *"Come/Sit/Stay"* commands. If your dog is not obeying your commands, you may not have taken the time to properly train them, or your energy may be too weak for them to respect you as a leader. This dog usually needs a firm leader, and without it he or she may take a stubborn, dominant attitude, while they ignore you and then soon become <u>your</u> leader.

If this is happening to you, get to work right away, step up your energy to ensure you are a strong enough leader, and train your dog so that everyone will be happy.

We all have our off days, so don't get down on yourself if you occasionally slip up and are not being as vigilant, strong and confident a leader as you need to be with this dog.

In a Nutshell

We humans will always have days when we are not as attentive as we need to be, which means that we will inevitably "slip up" sometimes when raising our fur friends.

What you need to remember is that it's not the end of the world, because there is always a solution, and often simply re-reading the relevant chapters in this book can quickly and easily get you back on track to raising a happy and well-behaved Labradoodle that is a pleasure to be around.

Also, it may help you to know that the familiar expression *"You can't teach an old dog new tricks"* is totally false. It doesn't matter what age a particular dog may be, because with patience and the right energy and knowledge, you absolutely CAN teach a dog of any age new tricks. It's just us humans that sometimes have difficulties learning new tricks.

Chapter 14: Surprise Bonus Chapter

*"Dogs have a way of finding the people
who need them, and filling an emptiness
we didn't ever know we had."*
— Thom Jones

If you thought that the end of this book was in view, well surprise, not quite yet, as I'd like to leave you with some canine wisdom and a short, funny, true story.

Happy Labradoodle Question and Answer Section

The following Q&A section is written from the dog's point of view, and although you may find it humorous, there are also valuable human lessons to be learned for anyone paying attention.

First, let me set the scene for the following situations:

This is a young, busy family, consisting of Mom and Dad, who work at home, one 12-year-old girl, and one 14-year-old boy, who share their lives with a 2-year-old dog named Sprocket. They all live together in a large house with a medium-sized, fenced yard out the back.

The following questions, asked by various members of the family, are directed to the dog, and answered by the dog, as if our dogs could actually talk like their humans.

Each question the dog answers is followed by a short review of the "lesson" we humans can learn from these various interactions.

Mom: **"Oh No! Why did you pee on the floor, Sprocket?"**

Sprocket: *"I'm sorry, I didn't mean to, but you forgot to let me out before you took the kids to school this morning, and I just couldn't hold it any longer."*

Lesson: Humans often lead very busy and distracted lives, and in order to ensure their dog remains happy, they still need to always pay attention, which often means putting their canine friend's needs ahead of their own.

Girl: **"Yuckeeee! Sprocket, why do you smell like dog poo?"**

Sprocket: *"I was chasing a rabbit in the back yard, and I guess those piles of doggy doo that the boy hadn't picked up yet got in the way."*

Lesson: Humans with convenient back yard doggy bathrooms often forget how important it is to regularly pick up the yard. This is not only a smelly bad habit that busy (or lazy) guardians can often be found guilty of, it's also a considerable health hazard that attracts rats.

Boy: **"What's wrong, Sprocket? You like to fetch — go get that ball!"**

Sprocket: *"Yes, I like to fetch, but it's hot out here, I'm getting exhausted and if I don't get water soon, I may pass out."*

Lesson: Sometimes we humans sharing our lives with dogs that have a passion for retrieving tend to forget that the temperature of the day may not seem extreme to us, but can can quickly become too much for a dog that is running back and forth fetching a ball while we're standing still.

We also forget that many dogs, despite their discomfort, have such a strong desire to retrieve and please their humans that they may continue to fetch that ball or Frisbee even though they may be about to collapse from heat exhaustion and are dying of thirst.

Dad: **"What happened in here, Sprocket! You've made a huge mess of all these boxes I had neatly stacked in the carport! What's wrong with you?"**

Sprocket: *"I saw a rat run in here and I was just trying to protect the home. I finally chased him out, and he won't be coming back. Sorry I knocked over the boxes."*

Lesson: Often we tend to quickly blame our canine friends when a mess is created for which there seems to be no logical explanation. We need to first think beyond simply blaming the dog for unexplained disarray, as there is often a good explanation that, in most cases, exonerates your canine companion.

Mom: **"Sprocket! What have you done? I left a plate of appetizers on the coffee table for our guests. Did you eat them?"**

Sprocket: *"Those pigs in a blanket smelled so good when I was passing through and couldn't resist. They were really tasty, but now I think I might have to throw up."*

Lesson: Many of our canine companions (such as the Labradoodle) don't know when to stop when it comes to filling their stomach. Therefore, if you have one of these dogs with an endless appetite for anything remotely resembling food, you need to be vigilant about never leaving human food, garbage or anything edible where they can reach it.

Boy: **"You bad, bad dog, Sprocket! You've chewed the laces off my expensive, new tennis shoes."**

Sprocket: *"But they smell just the same as those old shoes you gave me to play with, and now you're mad at me? I'm confused."*

Lesson: Think about what you allow your canine friend to play with, because giving them old discarded shoes, socks or other articles of clothing, etc., to play with can easily cause confusion in the canine mind when you get mad if they decide to chew your new shoes.

Girl: **"You're covering my bed in mud Sprocket! Get off!"**

Sprocket: *"But I like being next to you, and you let me sleep on your bed when I was a puppy, so please let me up."*

Lesson: If you'd rather not share your bed with a dog that could have just walked through a muddy puddle or rolled in a dead seagull, don't make the mistake of allowing them to sleep with you when they're a cute and much smaller puppy. If you do, it's unfair to blame your canine companion for wanting to continue this habit that you literally taught them.

Dad: **"Are you kidding me, Sprocket? Where's the hot dogs I left on the picnic table for the kids lunch?"**

Sprocket: *"Well, somebody forgot to feed me my breakfast and those hot dogs smelled so good that I couldn't resist. I'm sorry – I ate them while you were getting a beer. They were really good - got any more?"*

Lesson: Dogs are carnivorous and no matter their size, whether a tiny Chihuahua, a large Mastiff, or an agile and athletic Labradoodle, if given the opportunity, their desire to eat meat is a strong instinct you can't expect them to ignore. If you leave meat unattended, and your dog eats it, while someone may be at fault, it's not fair to blame your canine companion.

Moral of the Q&A section

Always DO pay attention to what your dog is trying to tell you, because (in addition to the above), there are so many other lessons we humans can learn from our beloved canine companions. Paying attention will help you to raise a Happy Labradoodle that will never have to experience unwanted behaviours.

There are so many lessons we humans can learn from our beloved canine companions IF we are paying attention.

Happy Labradoodle True Story

Before we close this Chapter, I hope you will enjoy the following true short story:

Ozzy's New Tiles

I was dog-sitting Ozzy, the Labradoodle, for clients of mine who had just recently installed a new tile entranceway in their home where previously there had been carpet tiles. The owners warned me that they were having a *"little problem"* getting Ozzy used to the new, shiny and quite slippery tiles and I told them not to worry about it, as I presumed this was a minor issue.

However, I soon found out that the joke was on me, because as soon as I had delivered the owners to the airport and returned to the home with Ozzy on leash at my side, I was brought to an abrupt halt when I opened the door and Ozzy flatly refused to enter the house.

Ozzy stopped so abruptly that the groceries I had been carrying became airborne and ended up strewn across the floor while it felt like I had become suddenly attached to a wriggling fire hydrant. OK, so much for the *"little"* problem Ozzy was having with the new flooring because there was no way he was going to put even one paw on those shiny new tiles.

Thank goodness it was a pleasant summer day because this was the perfect opportunity to start working out Ozzy's fear of this shiny new surface, which meant keeping the front door open.

I tied Ozzy's leash to the railing near the door, rescued my groceries from the tiled floor, found some of his favorite treats, and returned to untie Ozzy while I showed him I had something he wanted. He was immediately interested in the treats and started to follow me into the house only to put on the brakes at the edge of the tiles.

I went inside a couple of feet and sat down on the tiled surface, holding my hand out to offer him one of his treats. He stretched as far as he could without stepping on the tiles trying to get to the treat he really wanted, while I kept calmly encouraging him to move forward.

Finally, after several failed attempts to get him to put even one paw on the dreaded shiny surface, you could almost see his mind working as he completely flattened himself onto his belly and used his legs like a frog to *"swim"* his way across the tiles to get the treat I was offering.

This was definitely one of the funniest and most innovative things I had ever seen a dog do, but I had to be careful not to laugh because he needed me to be his strong and confident leader, so I stifled my laughter and praised him for being so brave and figuring out how to get his treat.

So now here was Ozzy flat on his belly in the middle of the shiny tile surface with his beloved carpeting about ten slippery tiles away. I stood up and moved farther into the house onto the carpeted area, still encouraging him to come and get another of his favorite treats.

He stared at me with those pleading eyes that seemed to say *"help me out of this predicament",* and all I could do was talk softly and confidently to him, pretending everything was just fine as I asked him to come and get another treat.

After a couple of minutes, Ozzy decided that the only way to get what he wanted was to *"swim"* a little farther as he flailed with his front paws and kicked with his back feet like a frog until he made his way onto the carpet, where he immediately bounded into life.

Stifling my laughter, I immediately praised and petted him, gave him several of his favourite treats, and all was now right in Ozzy's world, until it came time to go out for a lunchtime walk around the block.

I hitched up Ozzy's leash to his Martingale collar and started to walk toward the front door, which involved crossing over the tiled entranceway. I was hoping he would forget about his fear, but as soon as we reached the edge of the carpet, he immediately froze.

I stopped with him, keeping some forward tension on his leash, as I offered him a treat if he would just take one step onto the tiles. Instead, he immediately dropped onto his belly again, like a penguin about to slide down a snow bank, and started pushing himself across the tiles to get to the treat I was offering.

Such a sight he was and so determined to get his treat without having to walk – you had to give him credit for his amazing ingenuity.

When he got to my outstretched hand and gobbled down his treat, I gently picked him up and placed his feet onto the dreaded tiles where he stood in a crouched, unsteady position. Again, I encouraged him to walk toward me, and this time, although he remained crouched low, he gingerly attempted his first step, and then another and another until you could actually see a light bulb go off in his doggy brain when he realized that the smooth surface of the tiles was indeed safe to walk on.

I happily praised him for his bravery and gave him another treat, and then a few more times in and out the door and although he would slightly hesitate when stepping onto the tiles, and stoop down to sniff them, within three days of practicing our little routine, the dreaded slippery tile flooring no longer posed a problem for this smart and determined little dog.

When his owners returned from their holiday, you can imagine how happy they were to know that they no longer had to carry a 20-pound (9 kg) Ozzy across their entranceway.

Lesson to learn: **No matter the age of your dog, and how much you may have socialised them, when you change something in their world, they can become nervous, confused and traumatized. The only way to work through this is with much patience and understanding, coupled with persistent calm energy, and of course, their favourite treats.**

Published by Worldwide Information Publishing 2021

Copyright and Trademarks: This publication is Copyrighted 2021 by Worldwide Information Publishing. All products, publications, software and services mentioned and recommended in this publication are protected by trademarks. In such instance, all trademarks & copyright belong to the respective owners. All rights reserved.

No part of this book may be reproduced or transferred in any form or by any means, graphic, electronic, or mechanical, including photocopying, recording, taping, or by any information storage retrieval system, without the written permission of the authors. Pictures used in this book are either royalty free pictures bought from stock-photo websites or have the source mentioned underneath the picture.

Disclaimer and Legal Notice: This product is not legal or medical advice and should not be interpreted in that manner. You need to do your own due-diligence to determine if the content of this product is right for you. The authors and the affiliates of this product are not liable for any damages or losses associated with the content in this product.

While every attempt has been made to verify the information shared in this publication, neither the author nor the affiliates assume any responsibility for errors, omissions or contrary interpretation of the subject matter herein. Any perceived slights to any specific person(s) or organization(s) are purely unintentional. We have no control over the nature, content and availability of the web sites listed in this book.

The accuracy and completeness of information provided herein and opinions stated herein are not guaranteed or warranted to produce any particular results, and the advice and strategies, contained herein may not be suitable for every individual. The authors shall not be liable for any loss incurred as a consequence of the use and application, directly or indirectly, of any information presented in this work. This publication is designed to provide information in regard to the subject matter covered.

The information included in this book has been compiled to give an overview of the subject and detail some of the symptoms, treatments etc. that are available. It is not intended to give medical advice. For a firm diagnosis of any health condition, and for a treatment plan suitable for you and your dog, you should consult your veterinarian or consultant.

The writers of this book and the publisher are not responsible for any damages or negative consequences that may arise as a result of following any of the treatments or methods highlighted in this book.

Printed in Great Britain
by Amazon

59818154R00113